Atlanta
Running
Guide

Atlanta
Running
Guide

MIKE
COSENTINO

Ω

PEACHTREE

ATLANTA

FOR INGE

The best miles are the ones we cover together.
They are also the source of my inspiration for all of the others.

—M.C.

Ω

Published by
PEACHTREE PUBLISHERS, LTD.
1700 Chattahoochee Avenue
Atlanta, Georgia 30318-2112

www.peachtree-online.com

Text © 2003 by Michael Cosentino

Book and cover design by Loraine M. Joyner
Composition by Robin Sherman
Photographs: Ren Davis, Mike Cosentino,
          and MarathonFoto for the Atlanta Track Club

Manufactured in the United States of America
10 9 8 7 6 5 4 3 2 1
First Edition

ISBN 1-56145-205-X

Library of Congress Cataloging-in-Publication Data
Cosentino, Mike.
    Atlanta running guide / Mike Cosentino -- 1st ed.
        p. cm.
    Includes index.
    ISBN 1-56145-205-X

    1. Running--Georgia--Atlanta Metropolitan Area--Guidebooks. 2. Atlanta
Metropolitan Area (Ga.)--Guidebooks. I. Title.
GV1061.22 .C68 2003
796.42'09758'231--dc21
                                                            2002153456

TABLE OF CONTENTS

HOLIDAY TRADITIONS

APPENDIX

Textile mill ruins

along Sweetwater Creek

in Sweetwater Creek

State Park.

Preface

The idea for this book came to me as I was preparing for a friend and fellow runner to visit me in Atlanta. Planning to introduce him to running routes here, I realized there were too many wonderful places to run during a short visit. Since I knew this dilemma would arise again, I thought a guide to all of the great running places might be useful, both for me and for others.

When I began, I saw this book as an extension to my favorite hobby. Ultimately it proved to be the marriage of *two* of my interests—running and writing. The book provided the necessary extra motivation as I trained for the Western States 100-Mile Endurance Race. And writing about something I enjoyed was an ideal substitute for time I would have spent consuming ice cream or cold beer.

Then it happened. An evolution occurred. My project began to take on a life of its own. All of a sudden, I was getting up earlier than ever to re-run routes before work. During the early morning and evening hours of business trips, I was editing text instead of reading the newspaper or catching a few winks. On a cruise to South and Central America, I took my laptop out by the pool and studied maps of Atlanta. As with previous projects,

I refused to neglect my family and friends or my *real* job. Outside of those parameters, however, all bets were off.

It took more than 1500 miles on foot (and goodness knows how many more in the car and on my bike) before I finalized the 300 or more miles covered in this book. Believe me, not every mile you *can* run is a quality mile—visually or physically. Many more routes were considered than were included.

This book is by no means a complete listing of great runs in our city. Many people feel that the best runs are those where they discover something new on their own, an idea I fully understand. This guide is intended to turn you— whether you are a visitor, or new or longtime resident—on to places you may not have previously considered.

One of the benefits of running is that you can do it anywhere. I hope you will keep this guide near your shoes or in your car. If you do, you can in- crease your miles and your familiarity with our urban playground, often referred to as "Hot-Lanta," "The Big Peach," or "Capital of the South," and appropriately regarded as a runner's mecca. Enjoy!

The Peachtree Road Race ends in

Piedmont Park.

Acknowledgments

None of this would have been possible without my parents, Michael and Dianne Cosentino. Any good I ever do is the result of their love and encouragement, with which I have been blessed since my earliest days. I owe a huge thank-you to my brother, Tom, and to my dear friend since childhood, Craig Foy; they may not share all of my interests, but they always support them.

I must also acknowledge Scott Krizek, who turned me into the fanatic runner I am today. I *think* I am grateful for this. I hope Jason Pilarski, Pat O'Hare, and Bret Rachlin know how special they and their families are to me. Allowing me to share in their running triumphs is just one of many reasons why.

I want to gratefully acknowledge Jerry, Marijke, Monica, and Brent Campbell. Marrying into their family is blessing enough, but the interest they have taken in my own aspirations is also appreciated. Joe Szombathy is the greatest boss a man could ever hope to have. His guidance on the job and his support for my pursuits outside of it will never be forgotten.

This book may never have become a reality, and it certainly would not have been of the same quality, without Peachtree Publishers. The entire staff, and especially Lyn Deardorff, made invaluable contributions and made the writing *almost* as much fun as the running. Mark Morrison deserves all of the credit for the high-quality maps you find in this guide and an additional thank-you for his shared insights as a lifelong Atlantan.

I am grateful to the Atlanta PATH Foundation, not only for all the staff's assistance, but for their extensive and marvelous work providing paths for the pedestrians of Atlanta. Fran Poole was most helpful securing much-needed Atlanta-area Department of Transportation information. I also extend an overdue expression of gratitude to the many running clubs that helped me with research and were so very patient with my questions. Believe me, I would still be wandering around aimlessly on the golf cart paths in Peachtree City if it were not for the local club's assistance. And I would never have known how synonymous running clubs and fellowship could be without the South Fulton Running Partners.

Most importantly, I am infinitely grateful to my wife, Inge, for her unconditional love and unwavering support.

Introduction

This book was written for all runners in Atlanta, whether the newest participants or the most seasoned of harriers. Of course, not every suggestion is for everyone. That is why this guide tells you what lies ahead. You can choose what suits you, your time, your needs, and your mood.

HOW TO USE THIS GUIDE

The table of contents categorizes all of the runs by their location within or outside of the city of Atlanta, with the exception of the last two sections that describe trail running options and Atlanta's most popular races. While each route is different, they are all organized in the same manner, making it easy to match a route to your current skills and mindset. Further classification is available in the appendix.

Each entry contains the following information:

DISTANCE
Given in miles and kilometers.

HILL FACTOR
Atlanta is a city of hills, from rolling to steep. We've employed the following grading system:

NON-EXISTENT:
stretches flat as the local track
MILD:
requires a carpenter's level to detect
MODERATE:
proves variety is the spice of life
SIGNIFICANT:
needs oxygen supplements
EXTREME:
attracts those more stable physically than mentally

GETTING THERE
Directions to the recommended starting point or trailhead.

PARKING
Self-explanatory locations, usually at a church, shopping center, school, or other free space.

TRANSPORTATION
Public rail and bus transportation to the route, if available.

OVERVIEW
An explanation of why the entry made the *Atlanta Running Guide*. A brief history of the area, interesting facts, or a glimpse as to why the conditions are ideal for runners.

THE COURSE
The recommended running route, terrain, surface, and specific directions. Popular landmarks and notable obstacles are also included.

HIGHLIGHTS
Key visual, safety, and educational information and potential training benefits.

KEEP IN MIND
Information to help you determine if this run is for you, as well as hints for starting or finishing the run.

NEARBY NOTABLES
Pre- or post-run sites for hydration, food, rest-room visits, or rituals. Also offers ideas for places to meet your family or friends or to participate in area activities.

GENERAL INFORMATION

At the time of publication, no comprehensive local running book was available. There are, however, numerous publications and websites that address other running considerations, including training, diet, running clubs, races, apparel, and footwear suggestions. Although I recommend that you seek further information as needed, a few relevant topics are addressed here to help ensure that you get the most out of this guide.

GETTING STARTED

You've already heard this before: Before starting any new exercise program, consult your physician. It just makes sense that you'll enjoy the benefits of running more if you are sure it's conducive to your physical well-being.

After you get the green light from your doctor, you can increase your enjoyment of running by getting the right shoes *for you*. There is more to choosing the right shoes than just getting the same size as your Birkenstocks. You should also consider factors such as your foot shape, running mechanics, weekly mileage, and requirements for stability. The first time or two, you may wish to visit a running specialty store or a podiatrist to get an expert opinion on the right shoes.

VISITORS AND NEWCOMERS TO ATLANTA

Many visitors and new residents see runners everywhere in Atlanta. Almost 25 percent of the population consider themselves to be runners or joggers. In addition to the *quantity* of runners, Atlanta is also recognized for its *quality* of running. Longtime running residents were proud, but hardly surprised, to learn that in 2002, *Runner's World* magazine named Atlanta one of the "10 Best Cities To Be a Runner." Atlanta was the largest city to earn this distinction.

Many factors contribute to enjoyable running in Atlanta; some become increasingly evident the longer you run. Other factors bear mentioning before you start out.

This is the Sunbelt. We have plenty of sunny days that are warm or hot. Perspiration accelerates the effects of sun on your skin, so be sure to wear sunscreen. It might also be worth investing in a pair of sunglasses designed for runners.

You'll appreciate not squinting the entire way or having to wipe the sweat out of your eyes. Most importantly, remember that many days are very humid—and not just the sunny ones. The humidity can be more than 80 or 90 percent in the summer, so be sure to keep well hydrated. Finally, choose the time of the day to run based on your heat tolerance.

This is the South. In addition to the weather, people enjoy two other things about Atlanta: friendly people and the lush, green environment. As a runner in Atlanta, you can contribute to both traditions. Unless you are sucking wind terribly, offer a smile and greeting to those you pass. And when you take consumables with you on the run, please discard all refuse—water bottles, energy bar wrappers, gel containers—in trash receptacles. As the posted signs say, "Help keep Atlanta peachy clean!"

This is Appalachia. Actually, Atlanta is a bit southeast of Appalachia, but its topography is similarly diverse. There are rewards and challenges to running here. If you run the hills of Atlanta consistently and regularly, your body will learn to process oxygen more efficiently. The muscles in your calves and thighs will develop more quickly and noticeably. When planning a run, be sure to consider not only the distance, but also the hill factor. And don't count on running the same pace per mile on the streets as you do at the local track. If you are like many longtime Atlanta runners, you will eventually come to appreciate—rather than be intimidated by—the uneven layout.

TRAIL RUNNING

Trail running is an increasingly popular discipline within the sport of running, as demonstrated by the development of specific footwear and courses. Atlanta is not like the West when it comes to off-road running; there are not as many options available. But trail runners are not out of luck. Atlanta is ahead of most cities of its size in the availability and convenience of spacious and scenic trails. The Trailblazers section of this guide offers a wide range of options to get you started or keep you interested in this alternative. Keep the following in mind when running trails.

Trail Etiquette. As you come upon others, remember that they are probably moving more slowly than you. They may be out for a walk or a hike, more interested in the surroundings than you are, or with children or canine companions. *They have the right-of-way.* A friendly smile or polite "excuse me" is all you'll need to encourage most to step aside and let you by. You may need to use the side of the trail to get around a select few.

Mountain Bikers. You, as a trail runner, have the right-of-way. This doesn't do you much good, however, if you're lying on your back underneath a bike tire. Mountain bikes are not allowed on many trails in this guide. Use caution and common sense on those that are multiuse.

Sightseeing. The opportunity to see great natural beauty is one of the biggest benefits of trail running. Much can be absorbed whether you're on a leisurely stroll or clicking off six-minute miles. But if you are interested in looking more closely—really scrutinizing the environment—trail running is *not* the way to do it. Most injuries during trail running are the result of the runner taking his eyes off of the trail. If you spot something irresistible, take a breather.

ORGANIZED RUNNING AND RACING EVENTS

The vigor of Atlanta's running scene can be attributed to numerous factors, including a wide variety of organized events. In fact, there are more running events every year in Atlanta than in any other city in the United States. Exact dates and course layouts can change from year to year, so check regularly updated sources for the best information. The Atlanta Track Club website (www.atlantatrackclub.org) and the free local publications, *Atlanta Sports & Fitness* and *Georgia Athlete* magazines, are some of the best places to check.

The three most famous events— all held on major holidays—are the Peachtree Road Race, the U.S. 10K Classic, and the Atlanta Marathon & Half Marathon. Any runner that completes all of them has had a good year indeed. The Holiday Traditions section provides the race dates, course descriptions, and other pertinent information needed to get you started with your preparations.

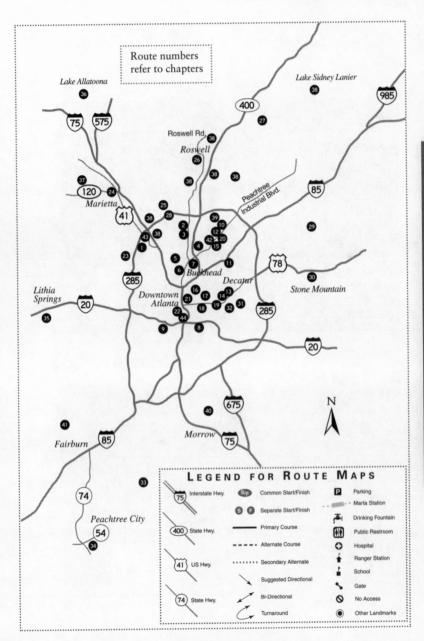

Route numbers
refer to chapters

Swan House at the Atlanta History Center.

(West Paces Ferry Route)

ATLANTA WEST

1

VININGS
Putting You through the Paces

DISTANCE
6.0 miles, 9.6 kilometers (loop)

HILL FACTOR
Significant

GETTING THERE
Approximately 9.0 miles north-west of downtown. Take I-285 to Paces Ferry Road (exit 18) and go east to Cumberland Parkway.

PARKING
Plenty of parking is available in the Paces Ferry Shopping Center at the intersection of Cumberland Park-way and Paces Ferry Road. Parking is also available along some of the side streets off Woodland Brook Drive.

PUBLIC TRANSPORTATION
The area is served by the #70 Cobb County Transit (CCT) bus, which departs from the Hamilton E. Holmes MARTA Station.

OVERVIEW
"Putting Yourself Through the Paces" is an apt title for this route, as you pass or use streets called Paces Ferry, Paces Mill, Paces Place, and Paces Walk. All are named after an early settler who built the area's first mill. And you'll literally feel the paces, as some of the climbs on this course are not for children. Nonetheless, the beauty of the residential portion makes this a run not to be missed for someone willing to—yes, you guessed it—get put through the paces.

The intersection of Paces Ferry Road and Cumberland Parkway is at the center of one of metro Atlanta's most rapidly expanding areas. Fortunately, the growth has not eroded the endear-ing characteristics of Vinings, nor has it discouraged the significant foot traffic the area has always enjoyed. Although the amount of activity in the area can be overwhelming at first, this location is actually a great place to run.

THE COURSE
MAIN ROUTE: The route begins at the intersection of Cumberland Park-way and Paces Ferry Road. Head east on Paces Ferry away from I-285. Cross the old railroad tracks and pass Paces Station, home to charming boutiques and restaurants. At the second traffic

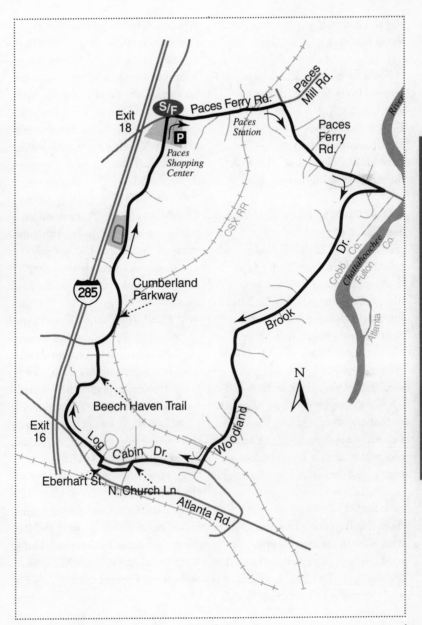

VININGS

signal, approximately 0.5 mile from the railroad tracks, Paces Ferry Road makes an abrupt right turn. If you see signs indicating you are now on Paces Mill Road, you have gone too far. Run downhill on Paces Ferry Road for almost another 1.0 mile, past many lovely houses. Turn right on Woodland Brook Drive at the traffic signal.

Follow Woodland Brook for about 2.0 miles and cross another set of railroad tracks. The road deadends at Log Cabin Drive; turn right and cross to the other side of the street to continue running on the sidewalk. The sidewalk ends 0.5 miles later at North Church Road. Turn left on North Church Road and go less than 100 yards to Eberhart Street, an unused road twenty yards south of and parallel to Log Cabin Drive. Eberhart ends all too soon, and Log Cabin Drive fills with automobile traffic. At this point, carefully use the side of the road to run the curves around several apartment complexes.

As you make your way north and back toward the starting point, the road changes name during the next few blocks to Beech Haven Trail and eventually becomes Cumberland Parkway at Gilmore Road.

Proceeding north on Cumberland Parkway, amid the areas obviously targeted for development, you encounter two killer hills. Turn right on Paces Ferry Road at the second apex, near the Paces Ferry Shopping Center, and head for home—but not before conquering another formidable ascent.

HIGHLIGHTS
Most of Paces Ferry Road is shaded by beautiful trees. Although many of the neighborhood roads are dead ends or cul-de-sacs, they are worth exploring.

KEEP IN MIND
Even though sidewalks are available and most drivers in the area are courteous, you should be extra attentive when near the intersection of Paces Ferry Road and Cumberland Parkway.

NEARBY NOTABLES
The Station at Vinings, near the first railroad crossing, offers plenty to delight local runners, including thin-crust pizza at the New York Pizza Exchange and Chinese cuisine at Uncle Wong's and Orient Express.

MOUNT PARAN
Runnin' on the Ridge

DISTANCE
11.0 miles, 17.6 kilometers
(out and back)

HILL FACTOR
Significant

GETTING THERE
Approximately 9.0 miles northwest of downtown.

To reach the northern starting point, take I-285 to Roswell Road (exit 25), and go south to Mount Paran Road.

To reach the southern starting point, take I-75 to Mount Paran Road (exit 256) and go south to Paces Ferry Road.

PARKING
Parking is available on many of the side streets along Mount Paran and in the lots of several churches along the road.

PUBLIC TRANSPORTATION
The area is served by the Sandy Springs (#5) MARTA bus, which departs from the Lindbergh Center and Dunwoody Stations.

OVERVIEW
If you are tired of climbing Atlanta's hills, reaching the apex only to begin the descent, this may be your kind of run. Mount Paran Road follows Mount Paran Ridge from Roswell Road to Paces Ferry Road; the ridge was a significant stronghold for Confederate forces during the Civil War. This route gets you to the top quickly, then keeps you there. No matter how appealing the concept of "start on top, stay on top" may be, do not assume that this means the road is flat. The ridge offers consistent, gently rolling terrain with grand houses and estates below.

THE COURSE
MAIN ROUTE: While you can start this route at either end, I suggest you begin at the intersection of Roswell Road and run southwest on Mount Paran Road; this will allow you to become somewhat familiar with the road before you encounter any significant traffic (unless you run during rush hours). The first mile is lined with very impressive houses. In mile 2.0, the road rolls a bit more and you pass

MOUNT PARAN

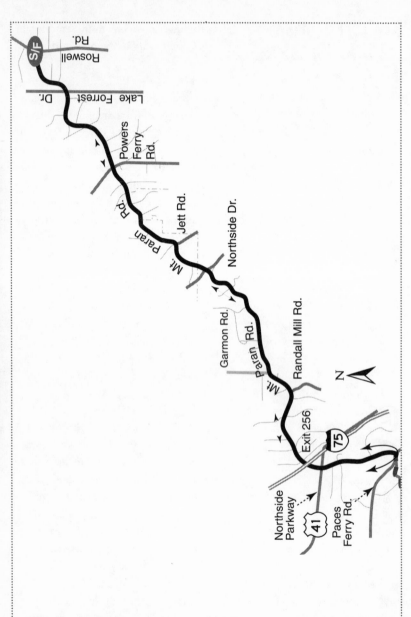

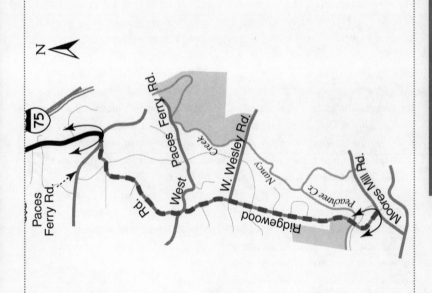

some more recent residential development and neighborhood churches, as well as the Mount Paran Country Store, which despite its busy suburban location is exactly what it sounds like. Cross under I-75 after 4.5 miles and go to the end of Mount Paran Road at Paces Ferry Road, exactly 1.0 mile later.

ALTERNATE: You can gain another pleasant 2.5 miles each way with significantly less traffic and significantly greater elevation by crossing Paces Ferry Road and continuing on Ridgewood (Mount Paran changes name to Ridgewood) to Moores Mill Road, then returning to the starting point.

HIGHLIGHTS
Despite the lack of provision for pedestrians in the original road design, Mount Paran Road is relatively safe. The winding nature of the road and the presence of many cyclists and pedestrians keep most drivers attentive. The side of the road has ample room to run (or bail out if necessary). A brief glimpse of the Buckhead skyline reminds you of the course's elevation. Many of the houses on this route are spectacular.

KEEP IN MIND
The course is frustratingly narrow in many areas and devoid of sidewalks or pedestrian/cyclist lanes almost the entire way. During the week, especially during the rush hours, traffic can quickly become bumper-to-bumper. Therefore, I recommend that you incorporate this run into your midday or weekend plans, so you won't have to deal with commuter traffic. The sidewalk under the I-75 entrance ramp can be very muddy; drivers are also much less attentive in this particular location. The steep hill near the intersection of Mount Paran and Paces Ferry Roads is a relatively brief exception to the gently rolling terrain.

NEARBY NOTABLES
The Mount Paran Country Store is a perfect place to buy a cold beverage or a snack. For more significant post-run sustenance, try any of the eateries in the Fountain Oaks or Chastain Square shopping centers, 0.5 mile and 1.0 mile, respectively, south of the intersection of Mount Paran and Roswell Roads.

CHASTAIN PARK
More Than a Walk in the Park

DISTANCE
4.0 miles, 6.4 kilometers (loop)

HILL FACTOR
Significant

GETTING THERE
Approximately 8.0 miles north of downtown. Take I-285 to Roswell Road (exit 25) and go south to West Wieuca Road, then west.

PARKING
Parking is permitted on West Wieuca Road in the park area and in the lots for the golf course, tennis center, and baseball/softball fields. Parking can be tricky at peak times and impossible on the evenings when the amphitheater is being used. Parking is not allowed on Lake Forrest Drive.

PUBLIC TRANSPORTATION
The area is served by the Chastain Park (#38) MARTA bus, which departs from the Lindbergh Center Station.

OVERVIEW
This area takes its recreation pretty seriously; it is home to a golf course, a tennis center, an arts center, a public swimming pool, an equestrian park, an outdoor amphitheater, baseball and softball fields, and a large playground. Chastain Park was formerly the site of a vicious Civil War battle in which hundreds of Confederate soldiers perished attempting to spurn the Federal advance into Atlanta. In recent years, the PATH Foundation, a nonprofit organization committed to building pathways throughout metro Atlanta, has constructed a wonderful route surrounding the park.

THE COURSE
MAIN ROUTE: This route begins at the corner of West Wieuca Road and Lake Forrest Drive. Follow the PATH signs south along Lake Forrest, circling the North Fulton Golf Course and passing a thriving wetland and natural wildlife habitat. At the 1.0-mile mark, take the pedestrian-only thoroughfare that branches off Lake Forrest Drive. This newly paved PATH portion concludes at the sidewalk on Powers Ferry Road on the west side of the golf course. Turn right and head north on the sidewalk, crossing

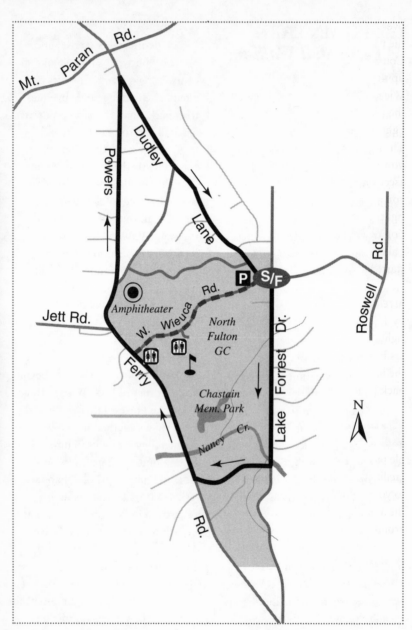

over Nancy Creek, and following the perimeter of the golf course. Continue past the tennis center and up the formidable hill to West Wieuca Road. At this intersection, the sidewalk ends, but the traffic is light and the sight lines are straight. The hill looming ahead of you, however, is a monster. A 0.5-mile ascent will leave you wheezing as you approach Dudley Lane. Turn right and descend to the intersection of West Wieuca Road and Lake Forrest Drive, where you started.

ALTERNATE: To decrease this route by 1.5 miles and avoid the hill, turn right on West Wieuca Road at Powers Ferry Road. This leads you past the baseball and softball fields and back to your point of origin.

HIGHLIGHTS
The sight of many other people using the park's recreational facilities provides an inspiring start to your run. There is plenty to do in the area for the non-runners in your group, whether adults or children.

KEEP IN MIND
Walkers, (some with strollers and dogs), cyclists, and in-line skaters also use the spacious paths.

No running is allowed on the golf cart paths. Because of the proximity of the route to the state's most popular city-owned golf course, you need to pay attention to the many "hackers" in the area and listen for their cries of "fore!" Traffic and parking can be challenging when a musical performance is scheduled in the amphitheater, so you may wish to check out schedules at www.atlantasymphony.org/chastain and www.atlantaconcerts.com/chastain.asp.

NEARBY NOTABLES
Rest rooms are located in the tennis center and the golf clubhouse. There is a large, popular playground just west of the intersection of West Wieuca and Lake Forrest intersection. The non-running members of your family can meet you for a post-run dive into the public pool, also located on West Wieuca Road. There are many food and drink establishments nearby in Buckhead.

4

WIEUCA ROAD
Where the Running Is Easy

DISTANCE
4.0 miles, 6.4 kilometers
(out and back)

HILL FACTOR
Mild

GETTING THERE
Approximately 8.5 miles northwest of downtown. Take I-285 to GA 400 South (exit 27) to the Buckhead Loop (exit 2) and go east (toward Peachtree Road). Immediately get in the far left lane and turn left on Phipps *Boulevard* (not *Drive*), then right on Wieuca Road.

PARKING
The large parking lot of the Wieuca Road Baptist Church can accommodate runners when church functions aren't scheduled. Plenty of free parking is available on the side streets along Wieuca Road or in the lots on the backside of Phipps Plaza. There are also multiple retail lots at the intersection of Wieuca and Roswell Roads where you can park before or after store hours.

PUBLIC TRANSPORTATION
This route is located near the Buckhead and Lenox MARTA Stations and is also served by the Peachtree Industrial (#25) MARTA bus, which departs from the Lenox Station.

OVERVIEW
Wieuca Road lies in perennial shade and in the shadows of the new monolithic condominiums of Buckhead. It's one of the area's best-kept running secrets. The stretch between Roswell Road and Peachtree Road covers 2.0 miles one way and is lined with wide pedestrian/cyclist lanes on both sides of the road. Completely residential, the road ambles through mature greenery, relatively light traffic, and infrequent hills.

THE COURSE
MAIN ROUTE: Start from the Wieuca Road Baptist Church on the pedestrian/cyclist lane and proceed north to Roswell Road, enjoying gradual descents most of the way. Of course, the opposite is true for the return, but neither direction merits much concern if you're accustomed to Atlanta roads. Most of the houses along Wieuca are on

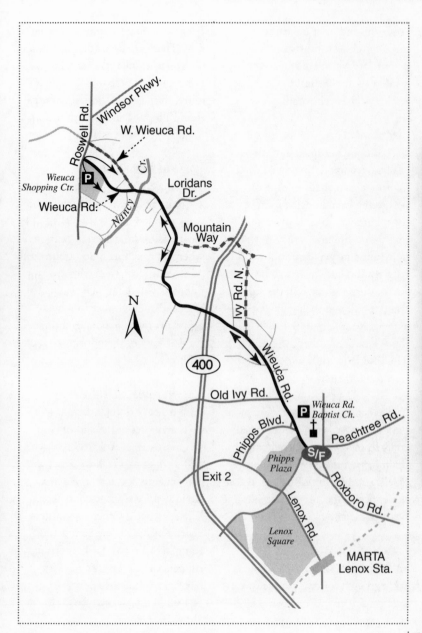

large lots and offer an attractive mix of architectural styles. The pedestrian/cyclist lane gives way to a sidewalk for the last 0.5 mile, ending at Roswell Road.

ALTERNATE: There are lots of side streets along the suggested route, easily accommodating those wanting to increase their mileage or peruse the local housing market on foot. For an enjoyable diversion on the southbound return, turn left on Mountain Way and follow the road until it ends at North Ivy Road. Turn right, climb the substantial hill, and then glide back to Wieuca Road, about 0.5 mile from the Wieuca Road Baptist Church. This alternate route adds about 1.0 mile to your run.

You can also connect with Chastain Park (entry 3). West Wieuca Road splits from Wieuca approximately 0.5 mile past the intersection of Wieuca and Roswell Roads and continues across the intersection into the heart of the park 1.0 mile later.

HIGHLIGHTS
The pedestrian/cyclist lane is wide enough for two people to run side-by-side in most places. The trees provide perfect protection from scorching summer sun or light rain. There are no traffic signals anywhere along this route. For non-running companions who are more proficient at shopping marathons, Phipps Plaza is within walking distance from start of this route.

KEEP IN MIND
In a couple of places the turns are quite tight, almost hairpins; be wary of oncoming traffic in these locations. Also, use extra caution when approaching automobiles and watch out for drivers who are mindlessly making their way onto Wieuca Road without looking, especially those making right-hand turns. Many of them forget to look both ways.

NEARBY NOTABLES
It's easy to replace your lost carbohydrates at the end of your run in this area. Atlanta's renowned and ultra-casual Fellini's Pizza is conveniently located on Roswell Road between Wieuca and West Wieuca Roads. Other suggestions nearby include Wing Swing and Kampai Sushi Bar. Early morning runners can find plenty of tasty bagels at Goldberg's Bagel Co. & Deli in the Wieuca-Roswell Shopping Center.

WEST PACES FERRY ROAD
A Run with a View

5

DISTANCE
6.0 miles, 10.0 kilometers
(out and back)

HILL FACTOR
Nonexistent

GETTING THERE
Approximately 6.5 miles north of downtown.

From the north, take I-285 to GA 400 South (exit 27) to the Buckhead Loop (exit 2) and go west to Piedmont Road, then south to Peachtree Road, then south to West Paces Ferry Road.

From the south, take I-75 to West Paces Ferry Road (exit 255) and go east to Peachtree Road.

PARKING
Plenty of parking lots are located near the many shops on both sides of West Paces Ferry Road. Give due consideration to the parking advisories posted. Parking is permitted along some of the side streets off West Paces Ferry.

PUBLIC TRANSPORTATION
The area is located near the Buckhead MARTA Station and is also served by the Lenox/Arts Center (#23) MARTA bus, which departs from the Lenox and Arts Center Stations.

OVERVIEW
Lined with multimillion-dollar homes and magnificent buildings such as the Georgia Governor's Mansion, the Cherokee Town Club, the Atlanta History Center, and Pace Academy, this stunning street grabs the attention of runners and non-runners alike. Throw in a flat, shaded route with ample sidewalks and lightly traveled footpaths and you have a runner's nirvana.

THE COURSE
MAIN ROUTE: Begin on the sidewalk on the north side of West Paces Ferry Road near the intersection of Peachtree Road and run west. After 0.5 mile, the sidewalk ends on this side of the street and begins on the other side. Cross to the south side and continue to Northside Parkway, where you turn around and return to the starting point. As a point of reference, your midway mark going either direction is roughly the Governor's Mansion.

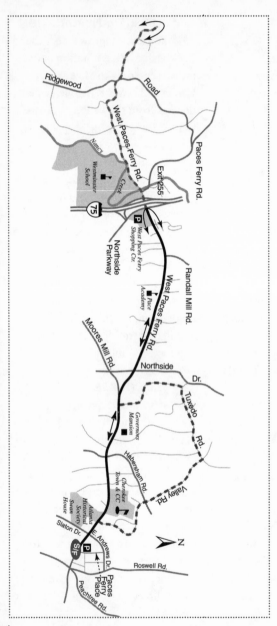

ALTERNATE: There are several side streets that offer lovely views of some of Atlanta's finest houses without the distraction of heavy traffic. To lengthen your run by almost a mile and experience this for yourself, go north on Tuxedo Road and follow to Valley Road. Turn right on Valley to get back to West Paces Ferry Road.

Another option is to continue on West Paces Ferry Road to the end and make the return for an additional 3.0 miles. The sidewalk ends and you encounter one monster of a hill, but you also gain an extra 1.5 miles (one way), a soft asphalt surface, and less traffic. And believe it or not, the residential scale is even more opulent. West Paces Ferry ends with a sign indicating "Private Drive."

HIGHLIGHTS
Large trees shade much of the course. There are commercial ventures and fast-food/casual dining options on either end of this route that provide convenient rest room locations. If you do this course during rush hour, you'll feel like a speed merchant as you get to I-75 from the Governor's Mansion before many of the cars do.

KEEP IN MIND
There is a stretch of road where the sidewalk gives way to a footpath, and both can be a bit rough in places. Traffic congestion is high during rush hours. Although traffic from the side streets is light, many drivers do not seem to expect pedestrians.

NEARBY NOTABLES
At the start of this route, there are a few dining establishments before the route turns completely residential. La Madeleine, a local chain known for its baked goods, offers inexpensive good food, coffee, and wine in a casual atmosphere. Near the intersection of Peachtree Road, there are a large number of food and drink options, including coffee shops and al fresco dining and drinking spots.

6

BUCKHEAD
Tracing the Battle Lines

DISTANCE
6.5 miles, 10.4 kilometers (loop)

HILL FACTOR
Significant

GETTING THERE
Approximately 0.5 mile north of downtown.

To reach the eastern starting point at the intersection of Rivers and Peachtree Battle Roads, take I-285 to GA 400 South (exit 27), to the Buckhead Loop (exit 2) and go west to Piedmont Road, then south to Peachtree Road, then southwest to Peachtree Battle Road, then west to Rivers Road.

To reach the western starting point at the intersection of West Wesley and Moores Mill Roads, take I-75 to Moores Mill Road (exit 254) and go west on Moores Mill Road to West Wesley Road.

PARKING
Plenty of free parking is available on Rivers Road, on the eastern part of Peachtree Battle Avenue, and on most of the side streets along the route. Parking is not permitted on West Wesley or Moores Mill Roads.

PUBLIC TRANSPORTATION
The area is located near the Buckhead MARTA Station and is also served by the West Wesley (#44) MARTA bus, which departs from the Lindbergh Center Station.

OVERVIEW
Another run in Buckhead? More gorgeous homes? Perfectly maintained lawns? Lush foliage? Well, yes, and then some! West Wesley Road and Peachtree Battle Avenue run practically parallel to one another in the heart of residential Buckhead. With rare exception, both of these roads have sidewalks, pedestrian/cyclist lanes, or footpaths, or are wide enough to accommodate runners *and* the light-to-moderate traffic. Be mindful, however, because the vehicle and pedestrian traffic becomes heavier during some parts of the day. The rather significant—if not downright disturbing—gradients are challenging for even the most aggressive hill-seeking runner.

BUCKHEAD

THE COURSE

MAIN ROUTE: Start your run where Peachtree Battle Avenue, Rivers Road, and Habersham Road meet, just west of the intersection of Peachtree Battle and Peachtree Road. Go north on tree-covered Rivers Road, which has a gradual uphill grade. Less than 0.5 mile later, Rivers Road ends at West Wesley Road. Turn left on West Wesley and head west for about 1.5 miles. Shortly after the Chatsworth subdivision, turn left on Moores Mill Road and take advantage of the pedestrian/cyclist lane for 0.5 mile. Make your final left turn at Peachtree Battle Road, and head east, for 2.0 miles back to the starting point.

ALTERNATE: Atlanta Memorial Park is located on Peachtree Battle Road at Northside Drive. The footpaths around the park's perimeter allow you to add up to 2.0 more miles to your run. If you prefer a wide-open, well-marked pedestrian/cyclist lane to the park, pass the starting point and turn left on Habersham Road and run to West Paces Ferry Road and back. Although the hills make the outbound run a challenge, this extension is a pedestrian-friendly, eye-pleasing trek that covers over 1.5 miles.

If you wish to shorten the basic route, take either Northside Drive or Howell Mill Road from West Wesley to Peachtree Battle. Although both options are relatively safe and short, they do not have pedestrian/cyclist lanes. Mileage is about 3.0 with Northside Drive and about 4.0 with Howell Mill.

HIGHLIGHTS

The architecture and landscape are magnificent. The easternmost mile on Peachtree Battle offers one of the best pedestrian/cyclist lanes in the city. This particular portion of the course is very popular with area runners. The distance and road conditions make this an ideal training run for your next Atlanta area 10K.

KEEP IN MIND

It is usually recommended that runners run against traffic. This advice is especially warranted on West Wesley Road where there are many blind curves. The run begins at the intersection of Rivers Road, Peachtree Battle Avenue, and

Habersham Road, but the sign for Rivers Road is obscured by foliage.

■ NEARBY NOTABLES

Peachtree Battle Promenade, just east of the starting point, offers dining options, including casual restaurants, a coffee shop, and an ice cream parlor. Or you can grab a quick beverage at a nearby gas station.

Atlanta Memorial Park

GARDEN HILLS and PEACHTREE HILLS
Zigzagging through the Neighborhoods

DISTANCE
4.5 miles, 7.2 kilometers
(out and back)

HILL FACTOR
Moderate

GETTING THERE
Approximately 5.5 miles north of downtown. Take I-285 to GA 400 South (exit 27) to the Buckhead Loop (exit 2) and go west to Piedmont Road, then south to Pharr Road, then west to Lookout Place.

PARKING
Frankie Allen Park, less than fifty yards from the suggested start of this route, has plenty of free parking, but can be congested on summer evenings because of youth baseball. Parking is also available on most surface streets within the neighborhoods.

PUBLIC TRANSPORTATION
The area is served by the Chastain Park (#38) MARTA bus, which departs from the Lindbergh Center Station.

OVERVIEW
Go right—and then take your first left. Repeat these directions every time you come to a T-intersection or a dead-end street to enjoy a beautiful, safe, and moderately challenging jaunt in what is arguably Buckhead's most under-appreciated area. The adjoining neighborhoods of Peachtree Hills and Garden Hills are close to some of Buckhead's most exclusive shopping and dining—as well as its loudest and most raucous nightspots—but the area is full of renovated bungalows and beautiful parks and gardens. The roads are wide, often lined by sidewalks, and free from the traffic snarls found nearby. Neighborhood streets create a seemingly incomprehensible maze that limits the opportunities for cars to cut through; only residents dare navigate the cul-de-sacs, dead ends, traffic circles, and the winding streets that change names. Just remember: "go right—and then take your first left."

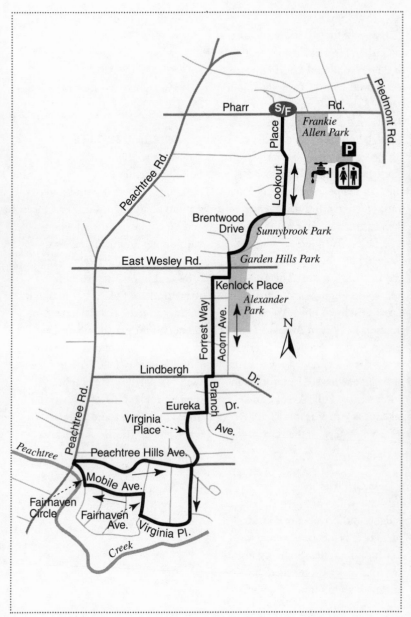

THE COURSE

MAIN ROUTE: This route starts in Garden Hills at the intersection of Pharr Road and Lookout Place, less than 0.25 mile from Piedmont Road. Take Lookout Place to Brentwood Drive and turn right. Turn right on Kenlock Place and left on Forrest Way. Turn right on Lindbergh Drive and run for fifty yards in the pedestrian/cyclist lane until you reach Branch Avenue, then turn left. Turn right on Eureka Drive. Turn left on Virginia Place, where there's a dry cleaner and two restaurants, The Treehouse and Philippe's Restaurant. Cross Peachtree Hills Avenue. Turn right on Fairhaven Avenue. Turn left on Mobile Avenue. Turn right on Fairhaven Circle. As you approach Peachtree Road, turn right on Peachtree Hills Avenue and take it back to Virginia Place. Retrace your steps to the start of the route.

HIGHLIGHTS

Sidewalks are plentiful, traffic is light, and drivers are considerate. There is plenty of shade for much of the route. Should you forget your instructions (as impossible as it may seem), most neighborhood residents are happy to point you in the right direction. In fact, they're quite used to doing so!

KEEP IN MIND

Go right—and then take your first left.

NEARBY NOTABLES

This route begins near Frankie Allen Park, which has tennis courts, ball fields, and playground equipment. Both Peachtree and Piedmont Roads are lined with dining and drinking establishments, including very casual cafes and bars. The Treehouse Restaurant & Pub has a small but wonderful deck that is perfect for runners. Enjoy a couple of drinks or their "continental cuisine with flair." You may feel more in tune with the patrons at Philippe's Restaurant, on the other hand, after you shower and change into some less athletic-looking attire.

GRANT PARK/
OAKLAND CEMETERY
Following in the Footsteps

DISTANCE
4.0 miles, 6.4 kilometers (loop)

HILL FACTOR
Moderate

GETTING THERE
Approximately 1.5 miles southeast of downtown Atlanta. Take I-20 to Boulevard (exit 59A) and go south to Grant Park.

PARKING
Plenty of free parking is available at the park and along many of the neighborhood streets.

PUBLIC TRANSPORTATION
The area is located near the King Memorial MARTA Station and is also served by the Lindbergh/Morningside/Grant Park (#31) MARTA bus, which departs from the Five Points Station.

OVERVIEW
Some people enjoy running in cemeteries; others don't. Without a doubt, cemeteries do offer well-maintained surfaces, quiet surround-

ings, and light traffic—favorable conditions for any runner. On the other hand, they can be disconcerting to some. If you can put aside your reservations about running in such a location, you'll find that Oakland Cemetery is not an ordinary burial ground. Atlanta's first public cemetery, it is the final resting place for many famous Atlantans, including author Margaret Mitchell, golfer Bobby Jones, and Moses Formwalt, the city's first mayor. Three thousand soldiers killed in the Civil War—including sixteen from the Union—are buried here, near a 65-foot obelisk honoring "Our Confederate Dead." If the history or the significance of those interred does not impress you, then perhaps the funerary art found on the monuments, markers, and mausoleums will.

Historic Grant Park—the larger part of this route—is equally wonderful for runners. Zoo Atlanta and the Atlanta Cyclorama, an extensive Civil War museum, are located in the park. The surrounding neighborhood was once the centerpiece of Victorian Atlanta and is now the picture of ongoing urban renaissance.

THE COURSE
MAIN ROUTE: Although you

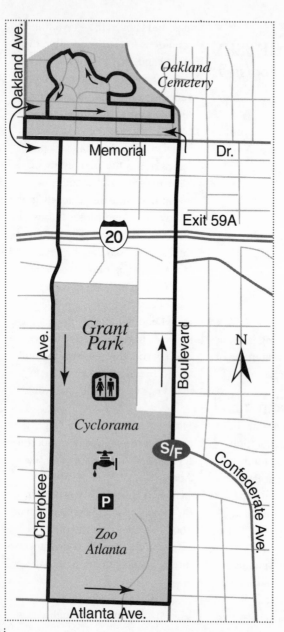

can begin on any of the roads surrounding Grant Park, I suggest you start on Boulevard, at the entrance into the largest parking lot. Since this route is almost perfectly rectangular, all you need to remember is that Oakland Cemetery is north of Grant Park.

From Boulevard, go north along the perimeter of the park. After 0.25 mile, leave the park area and cross I-20. (Although this interchange is often congested, sidewalks and traffic signals ensure a safe crossing.) The next .25 mile descends to Memorial Drive, where you will see the brick walls and sidewalks of Oakland Cemetery. Cross Boulevard and turn left on Memorial. The brick-paved sidewalks rise gradually for 1.0 mile along the old cemetery walls. At Oakland Avenue, turn right through the barriers that prevent cars from entering the cemetery. The main entrance into the cemetery is one hundred yards to the north.

Once inside the cemetery, take the path from the entrance to the end of the main thoroughfare. Go left and follow the outer contour of the cemetery back to where you started. You have covered almost

exactly 1.0 mile. (There are plenty of other routes you can take inside the cemetery.)

Exit the cemetery at the main gate, cross Memorial Drive and head south on Cherokee Avenue. (The sign for this street is only on the opposite side of the street.) The road gently rises and falls as it crosses back over I-20 and passes some fabulously restored Victorian houses. As you continue south past the neighborhood boutiques and back into the park area, the incline becomes more challenging. From this side of Grant Park, there are wonderful views of the Zoo, the neo-classic Cyclorama, and the park itself. After the first mile on Cherokee Avenue, turn left on Atlanta Avenue and begin a formidable 0.3 mile climb to Boulevard. Turn left to arrive back at your point of origin at the main entrance to Grant Park.

ALTERNATE: The interior roads of Grant Park offer more miles to run. If you don't wish to run through the cemetery, don't cross Memorial Drive. Instead, turn left on Memorial and then left on Cherokee Avenue. Excluding the cemetery decreases the distance of this route by 1.0 mile.

HIGHLIGHTS

There are sidewalks along the entire route. Zoo Atlanta, the Cyclorama, and Oakland Cemetery provide plenty of activities for the non-runners in your group. Markers in Oakland Cemetery indicate the headstones of the most notable residents.

KEEP IN MIND

The park closes at 11:00 PM. Be careful, particularly after dark; though this colorful historic area is experiencing rejuvenation, it is still wise to keep your personal safety in mind.

NEARBY NOTABLES

Six Feet Under, located on Memorial Drive across from Oakland Cemetery, serves a casual seafood menu in a pub atmosphere. On a nice day, enjoy their rooftop deck, which provides a view of downtown Atlanta. Ria's Bluebird Café, on Memorial Drive at Cherokee Avenue, is a down-home diner that also prepares food to go. Within Grant Park is a McDonald's for quick drinks, meals, and the code for access to the rest room. Park Point Community Grocery is nearby at the corner of Atlanta Avenue and Cherokee, adjacent to the Atlanta Police precinct.

Grant Park neighborhood

WESTVIEW CEMETERY
Running in Peace

DISTANCE
5.0 miles, 8.0 kilometers
(double loop)

HILL FACTOR
Mild

GETTING THERE
Approximately 3.5 miles west of downtown. Take I-20 to Martin Luther King Jr. Drive (exit 53) and go east for less than 0.25 mile, then south on Ralph David Abernathy Boulevard to Westview Drive.

PARKING
Parking is permitted on all cemetery roads. Lots are located near the chapel and at the mausoleum.

PUBLIC TRANSPORTATION
The area is located near the West End MARTA Station and is also served by several MARTA buses, including Auburn Avenue/ Martin Luther King Jr. (#3), which departs from the Hamilton E. Holmes and Five Points Stations, and Beecher (#64), which departs

from the West Lake Station.

OVERVIEW
Running in a cemetery may not be for everyone, but some feel that the solitude and serenity outweigh the constant reminder of our mortality. Though other routes in this book may incorporate graveyards, this is the only one that is located entirely within a cemetery. Westview is the biggest cemetery in Atlanta and one of the largest in the South. Perhaps more importantly for runners, the interior roads are wide, lightly traveled, and well maintained. This makes it easy to get in as many miles as you wish.

THE COURSE
MAIN ROUTE: The most popular route is a loop road. At the first road inside the main entrance, take either a left or right turn and follow the perimeter of the cemetery on the outermost roads. You realize how enormous this place is when you discover that this roadway alone covers 2.5 miles! It also brings you back to the main entrance without any guesswork

ALTERNATE: If you are feeling a bit more adventurous, there are dozens of additional miles to be

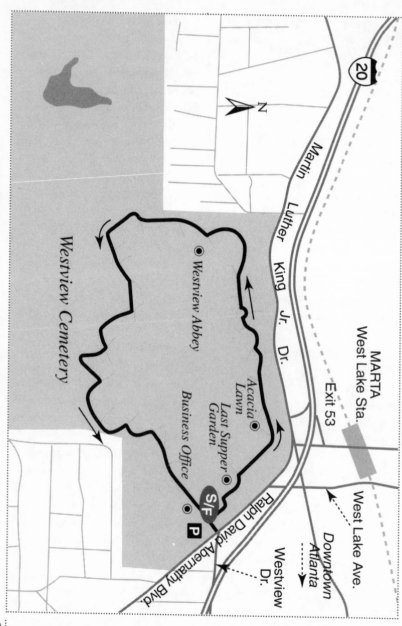

20

N

Martin Luther King Jr. Dr.

Westview Cemetery

Westview Abbey

Acacia Lawn

Last Supper Garden

Business Office

S/F

P

MARTA
West Lake Sta.

Exit 53

West Lake Ave.

Downtown Atlanta

Westview Dr.

Ralph David Abernathy Blvd.

run using interior roads. Note how much of the cemetery is currently unused. In these areas, it's almost like a city park. An elaborate mausoleum—the largest in the state of Georgia—is located on one of these interior paths.

HIGHLIGHTS

Though Westview is within 0.5 mile of the intersection of I-75/85 and I-20, it is still one of the few places in downtown Atlanta where you can completely escape what some might consider to be urban perils. Plenty of spigots make it easy to refill your water bottle.

KEEP IN MIND

The official hours—8:30 AM to 5:30 PM daily—are somewhat restricting. The only available rest room is in the abbey near the mausoleum. Westview Cemetery is safe, but is located in a somewhat unpredictable area of Atlanta.

NEARBY NOTABLES

Hard-earned miles in the cemetery may leave you feeling somewhat lifeless, but a liquid resurrection in the form of the best smoothies in town is available less than 1.0 mile away at the Mutana Health Café at Ralph David Abernathy Boulevard near Cascade Road.

The Virginia-Highland

neighborhood

ATLANTA EAST

PEACHTREE DUNWOODY
Pushing Pill Hill

DISTANCE
7.0 miles, 11.2 kilometers
(out and back)

HILL FACTOR
Extreme

GETTING THERE
Approximately 8.0 miles northeast of downtown. Take I-285 to GA 400 South (exit 27) to the Buckhead Loop (exit 2) and go east to Peachtree Road then north to Peachtree Dunwoody Road.

PARKING
Parking is available on Peachtree Dunwoody Road at Wendover Lane, 300 yards from the southern starting point. Parking for the northern starting point is available on Clementstone Drive, the first side street, as well as on many of the other side streets.

PUBLIC TRANSPORTATION
The area is served by the Peachtree Industrial (#25) MARTA bus, which departs from the Lenox Station.

OVERVIEW
Peachtree Dunwoody Road, from Peachtree Road to the Glenridge Connector, features 3.5 miles of undulating hills, attractive homes, and tempting side streets, as well as a pedestrian/cyclist lane and enough trees overhead to keep you in the shade the entire way. Sound easy? Don't be fooled. This route is not for wimps; the hills are demanding. In fact, this jaunt may leave you feeling grateful that the turnaround point is within sight of several hospitals.

THE COURSE
MAIN ROUTE: Many Atlantans will tell you that the local running scene begins and ends at Peachtree Road (entry 20). This route does just that, starting and ending on Peachtree Road, at the Peachtree Dunwoody intersection. Although starting from the southern end gets the most challenging part out of the way first, that doesn't mean that the way back is easy. The first mile starts on a descent and covers a couple of relatively minor downhill slopes, but the majority of the distance is uphill. The last three-quarters of this introductory mile threatens to separate your lungs

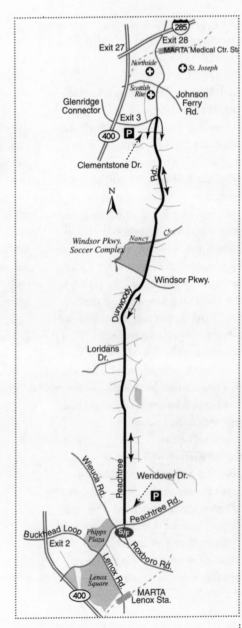

from your chest. And once you reach the summit, the next 1.5 miles goes just as cruelly downhill.

At 1.5 miles, the pedestrian/cyclist lane is at its narrowest. There is no sidewalk here, and the road winds significantly, so be extra mindful of traffic. At 2.0 miles, you come to Windsor Parkway, the only major intersection on this route and the site of the expansive Windsor Parkway Soccer Complex. This is also the beginning of the only flat part of your trip. Be sure to enjoy it because 0.5 mile later, you begin the grueling climb up Pill Hill that takes you past the 3.0-mile mark at Northside Community Church and up to the conclusion of the route at the Glenridge Connector. I don't recommend running beyond this intersection because the pedestrian/cyclist lane and sidewalks end and the traffic intensifies.

HIGHLIGHTS
If you don't want a flat course, you've come to the right place. The entire route is residential. The traditional elegance of older residences is complemented by the grandeur of many of the newer homes. There is little need for sunglasses as the entire route is beneath a canopy of trees.

KEEP IN MIND
Although a model for other Atlanta thoroughfares, the pedestrian/cyclist lane is narrow in certain areas.

NEARBY NOTABLES
Ice cream lovers, your reward for completing this difficult course is close by. Try the Marble Slab Creamery across the street from the starting point or Bruster's Old Fashioned Ice Cream & Yogurt in Cherokee Plaza center, about 0.5 mile north. If you need a warm-up before the ice cream, Mellow Mushroom Pizza Bakers and Jocks N Jills Sports Grill are less than 1.0 mile north on Peachtree Road.

11

SAGAMORE HILLS
More Ups and Downs

DISTANCE
5.0 miles, 8.0 kilometers (loop)

HILL FACTOR
Extreme

GETTING THERE
Approximately 8.5 miles northeast of downtown. Take I-85 to Clairmont Road (exit 91) and go south to Briarcliff Road, then east to Fisher Trail.

PARKING
Parking is permitted on Fisher Trail.

PUBLIC TRANSPORTATION
The area is served by the Briarcliff (#33) MARTA bus, which departs from the Lindbergh Center and Chamblee Stations.

OVERVIEW
This residential loop is perfect for those who want hills with equal numbers of ascents and descents. It's also the closest thing to a perfect circle you can find. Unfortunately, street name changes and unavoidable short stints on a couple of roads make the description sound rather complicated. Rest assured, though, one time through and you won't forget this route.

THE COURSE
MAIN ROUTE: Although you can start this route at any point, I suggest you start at the intersection of Briarcliff Road and Fisher Trail. Head north on Fisher, which will change names twice in 1.5 miles, to Meadowvale Drive, then Heritage Drive, before it meets Briarcliff Road again. Turn left on Briarcliff Road and go one block to Oak Grove Road. Turn right on Oak Grove and go to LaVista Road. Turn right again.

Although your good judgment as a runner tells you to run against traffic, resist that thought here. After one short block, turn right onto Alderbrook Road. Running with the traffic here keeps you from having to cross over LaVista twice in just 200 yards. Watch for the intersection of Alderbrook and Ravenwood Way next to Sagamore Hills Elementary School. Alderbrook Road splits off wildly to the left and eventually ends. Follow the signs for Ravenwood Way to

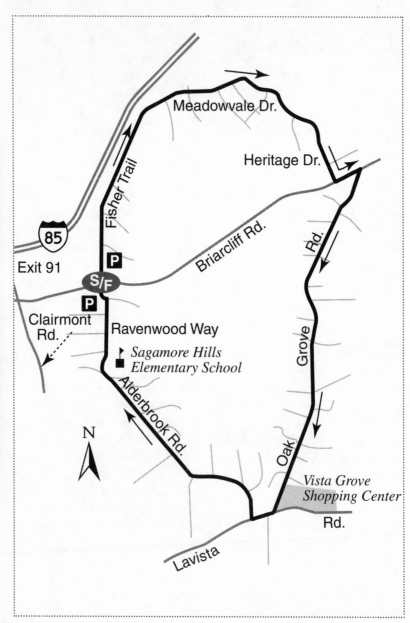

SAGAMORE HILLS

Meadowvale Dr.

Heritage Dr.

Fisher Trail

85

Exit 91

P

S/F

P

Clairmont Rd.

Ravenwood Way

Sagamore Hills Elementary School

Briarcliff Rd.

Rd.

Grove

Oak

Alderbrook Rd.

N

Vista Grove Shopping Center

Rd.

Lavista

complete your trip back to Fisher Trail. At Fisher Trail, turn left and return to the intersection where you started.

HIGHLIGHTS

Most of the hills are long slopes rather than steep inclines. With rare exception, the course offers a sidewalk, a pedestrian/cyclist lane, or a quiet neighborhood street.

KEEP IN MIND

The use of some of the sidewalks or pedestrian/cyclist lanes requires crossing the road in awkward intervals; do so with caution. The hills along this route are challenging and feel almost never-ending.

NEARBY NOTABLES

There are many options for food and drink at the Briarcliff and Clairmont Road intersection. Mo's Pizza can satisfy any pizza fanatic. Mimi's in a Minute Gourmet Café has a nice selection of sandwiches. Madras, an Indian vegetarian restaurant, and Sidelines Sports Bar & Grill are located in the Williamsburg Village Shopping Center. Mocha Delight can provide quick "pick-me-ups" at their drive-in window. Ed's IGA grocery provides pre- or post-run necessities.

BROOKHAVEN
Playing through the Course

DISTANCE
3.0 miles, 5.0 kilometers (loop)

HILL FACTOR
Moderate

GETTING THERE
Approximately 8.5 miles northeast of downtown. Take I-285 to GA 400 South (exit 27) to the Buckhead Loop (exit 2) and go east on the Buckhead Loop to Peachtree Road, then north to Brookhaven Drive.

PARKING
There is plenty of parking in lots near the intersection of Peachtree Road and Brookhaven Drive, but be wary of business owners who take towing of non-customers seriously. Parking is not allowed on any of the streets along this route. There is a small off-road parking area on East Club Drive, just west of the East Brookhaven Drive intersection.

PUBLIC TRANSPORTATION
Brookhaven Drive is across the street from the Brookhaven/ Oglethorpe University MARTA Station.

OVERVIEW
Established in 1911, Georgia's oldest golf community has well-maintained roads, relatively light traffic, and magnificent homes boasting remarkable golf course views. Many Atlantans consider this one of the area's most beautiful neighborhoods. If you are loath to add miles by repeating the same route, this course around the Capital City Country Club may change your mind. This is a popular area for runners and walkers, whom you're sure to encounter most every evening and weekend.

THE COURSE
MAIN ROUTE: This route begins at the intersection of Brookhaven Drive and Peachtree Road. Take Brookhaven Drive, which circles the golf course, and veer left or right at the first intersection. Proceed approximately 1.0 mile to Club Drive. Go left if you first veered right and right if you first veered left. Pay close attention to the road signs to be sure that you

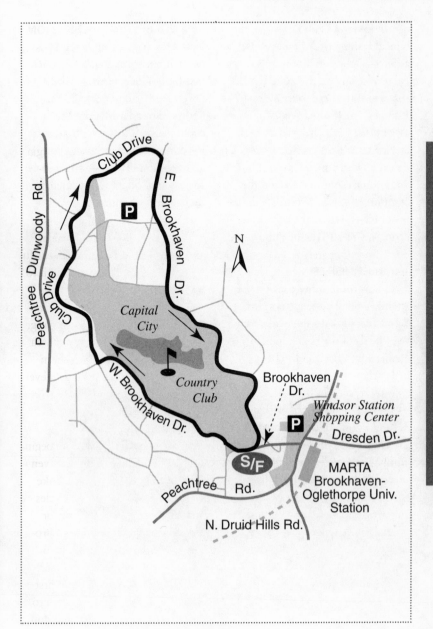

are, indeed, on Club Drive. (In the typical fashion of Atlanta roads, going straight does not necessarily mean you stay on the same road.) Also resist the urge to turn down East or West Club Drive. After another mile, Club Drive leads back to East or West Brookhaven Drive, depending on which way you initially went. Continue around the contours of the golf course back to Brookhaven Drive, the road that brought you into the neighborhood.

HIGHLIGHTS

This route showcases one of Atlanta's finest residential areas. While there are no sidewalks for two-thirds of the route, most drivers here are very mindful of pedestrians.

KEEP IN MIND

No running is permitted on the golf course, including golf cart paths. The terrain is rolling and there are two formidable hills.

NEARBY NOTABLES

This area is completely residential, but there are a number of fast-food outlets nearby on Peachtree Road. A Jocks N Jills Sports Bar and a Mellow Mushroom Pizza Bakers are situated at the corner of Brookhaven Drive and Peachtree Road—and don't be surprised to find a lot of runners there ahead of you.

MASON MILL
Magnificent Miles

DISTANCE
3.75 miles, 6.0 kilometers
(out and back)

HILL FACTOR
Significant

GETTING THERE
Approximately 5.0 miles northeast of downtown. Take I-85 to Clairmont Road (exit 91) and go south to Mason Mill Road, then east to the DeKalb County Sports and Tennis Center.

PARKING
Plenty of free parking is available at the tennis center.

PUBLIC TRANSPORTATION
The area is served by the Clairmont Road (#19) bus, which departs from the Decatur and Brookhaven Stations.

OVERVIEW
The DeKalb Tennis Center is tucked behind Clairmont Road in Mason Mill Park. It's one of the city's best-kept recreational secrets, offering more than a dozen tennis courts, a large playground, a baseball field, and a public gym. The secret may soon be out, however, as the area is undergoing significant development. It's the perfect place to begin a jaunt on the nearby roads that boast some of Atlanta's best-maintained and most accommodating sidewalks.

THE COURSE
MAIN ROUTE: From the tennis center, head west on McConnell Drive toward Clairmont Road. Turn left at the Avis G. Williams Library. Cross Clairmont and continue on McConnell for another 0.5 mile to Mason Mill Road. Turn right on Mason Mill and begin a series of winding and steep quarter-mile climbs. This is your initial oxygen check. Cross Houston Mill Road and enter the Victoria Estates community. The road descends and, of course, ascends for another 0.5 mile through a valley filled with attractive houses and expertly maintained lawns. Mason Mill Road eventually terminates at the 2.0-mile mark at Rainer Falls Drive. Turn right. You're not out of the woods yet, literally or figuratively. In fact, the beauty of the neighborhood could be

MASON MILL

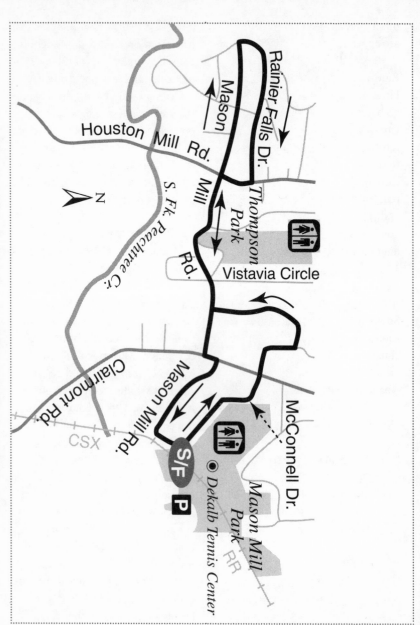

offset by the horror of the hill you are approaching.

Rainer Falls Drive ends back on Houston Mill Road. Turn right and go back to Mason Mill Road. Cross back over Houston Mill and return to the park on Mason Mill Road. Instead of picking up McConnell Drive at the bottom of the hill, continue on Mason Mill Road and cross Clairmont. It will take you into the park, completing this figure-eight-shaped course.

HIGHLIGHTS
There are excellent sidewalks on even the busiest roads. Rest rooms are located at the tennis complex and at W. D. Thomson Park, which is north of Mason Mill Road, just west of Vistavia Circle.

KEEP IN MIND
A couple of the Mason Mill Road intersections can be very busy; use the signals and crosswalks.

NEARBY NOTABLES
While this area is exclusively residential, nearby Toco Hill Shopping Center offers a number of fast-food outlets, a variety of moderately priced restaurants, and two large grocery stores.

EMORY/ DRUID HILLS
Climbing Clifton

DISTANCE
8.0 miles, 12.8 kilometers
(out and back)

HILL FACTOR
Extreme

GETTING THERE
Approximately 5.0 miles
northeast of downtown.

To reach the northern starting point
at the intersection of Briarcliff Road
and Clifton Road, take I-85 to
North Druid Hills Road (exit 89),
and go east to Briarcliff Road, then
south to Clifton Road.

To reach the southern starting point
at the intersection of Ponce de Leon
Avenue and Clifton Road, take
I-75/85 to North Avenue/Georgia
Tech (exit 249D) and go east to
Moreland Avenue, then north to
Ponce de Leon Avenue, then east to
Clifton Road.

PARKING
There is plenty of free parking
at Sage Hill Shopping Center at the
intersection of Clifton and Briarcliff
Roads. On the southern end,
parking is available at the Fernbank
Museum of Natural History and on
certain side streets. Most of the
parking at Emory University is by
permit only.

PUBLIC TRANSPORTATION
The northern starting point is
served by several MARTA bus
routes, including Emory (#6), which
departs from the Edgewood/Candler
Park and Lindbergh Stations, and
Thomasville/Lenox (#48), which
departs from the Inman Park/
Reynoldstown and Lenox Stations.
The southern starting point is
served by the Ponce de Leon (#2)
MARTA bus, which departs from
the North Avenue Station.

OVERVIEW
This run takes you into the
heart of the Emory University campus and past the home of the president at Lullwater Park. The sidewalks on the east side of Clifton
Road were initially constructed by
area developers because of the
Emory University setting. This
pedestrian passage is now a legacy
available to everyone. Brave is the
harrier who tackles the elevation
changes on this route, for the hills

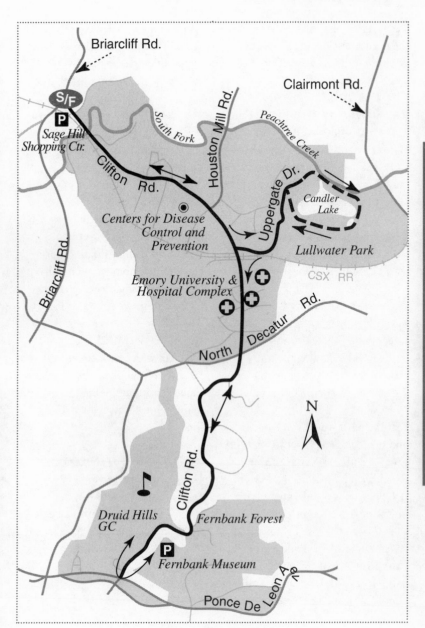

Briarcliff Rd.

Clairmont Rd.

S/F

P

Sage Hill Shopping Ctr.

South Fork

Houston Mill Rd.

Peachtree Creek

Clifton Rd.

Uppergate Dr.

Candler Lake

Centers for Disease Control and Prevention

Lullwater Park

Briarcliff Rd.

CSX RR

Emory University & Hospital Complex

North Decatur Rd.

N

Clifton Rd.

Druid Hills GC

Fernbank Forest

P

Fernbank Museum

Ponce De Leon Av.

are never-ending. As compensation, the road offers plenty of beauty in addition to its fitness benefits.

THE COURSE

MAIN ROUTE: This route begins at the intersection of Briarcliff and Clifton Roads. Head southeast on Clifton down an extremely demanding hill, past the Centers for Disease Control and Prevention and the Emory Conference Center Hotel. At the pinnacle, a little over 1.0 mile from the beginning, you reach Lullwater Park, one of the most runner-friendly places in Atlanta. Home to the president of Emory University, the park is open to the public and rarely busy. An easy-to-follow loop in the park, including the trail around the lake, provides you with 2.0 idyllic, automobile-free miles.

Exit the park where you entered and turn left. The Emory University campus ends at North Decatur Road, the first major intersection. Another series of hills awaits you on the next section of Clifton Road, as you pass lovely bungalows and lavish estates. When you see Fernbank Museum of Natural History and Druid Hills Golf Club, you're almost at the end of the route at Ponce de Leon Avenue. Turn around and head back to the starting point, bypassing Lullwater Park to achieve the mileage listed above.

ALTERNATE: Other trails in Lullwater Park offer additional distance and ultimately return to the main thoroughfare.

HIGHLIGHTS

There is an amazing view of the midtown and downtown skylines from Clifton Road. Emory University is home to many lovely historic buildings. There are emergency phones in Lullwater Park.

KEEP IN MIND

Lullwater Park closes at dark. Be wary of mindless drivers who pull out without looking from the many Emory University parking lots.

NEARBY NOTABLES

At the intersection of North Decatur and Oxford Roads, Emory Village features a number of cafes, including Everybody's Pizza. Most area restaurants have outdoor seating.

DREW VALLEY
High Grades without Studying

DISTANCE
1.7 miles, 2.7 kilometers (loop)

HILL FACTOR
Moderate

GETTING THERE
Approximately 8.5 miles northeast of downtown. Take I-85 to North Druid Hills Road (exit 89) and go west to Buford Highway, then turn left and go to Drew Valley Road.

PARKING
You can park anywhere on Drew Valley Road as well as on any of the available side streets.

PUBLIC TRANSPORTATION
The area is served by several MARTA bus routes, including Buford Highway (#39), which departs from the Lindbergh and Doraville Stations, and Chamblee (#70), which departs from the Brookhaven/Oglethorpe University and Chamblee Stations.

OVERVIEW
This Brookhaven neighborhood offers a wonderful, relatively short loop, perfect for those runs often reserved for the local track. There are no traffic signals or busy intersections, but the ease of performing multiple laps should not make you think that this is an easy run. Unlike the local track, Drew Valley Road has elevation changes that cannot be taken lightly.

THE COURSE
MAIN ROUTE: Begin at the intersection of Drew Valley and East Drew Valley Roads, going west on Drew Valley. The first mile offers gradual and then quite pronounced (as much as 15 percent) descents. After the initial mile, a dastardly duo of valleys, including Drew Valley itself, collaborate to test your quads and calves. At the apex of the second hill, you're back at East Drew Valley. Turn right to return to your point of origin.

HIGHLIGHTS
This neighborhood offers lush greenery in the spring and brilliant

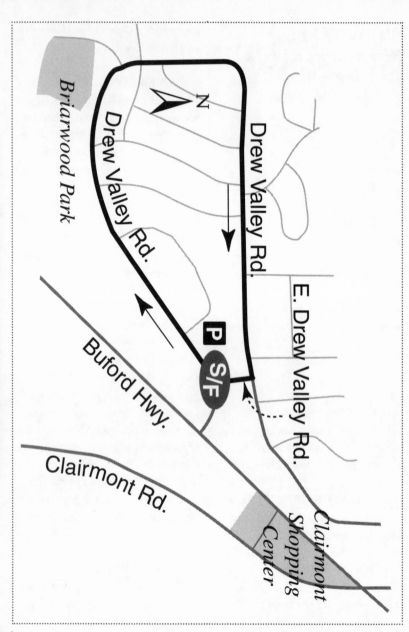

Briarwood Park

Drew Valley Rd.

N

Drew Valley Rd.

E. Drew Valley Rd.

Buford Hwy.

P

S/F

Clairmont Rd.

Clairmont Shopping Center

fall foliage. Numerous side streets, including Burch Circle, Poplar Springs Drive, and Nesbitt Drive, all neatly intersect the Drew Valley lap. Traffic is light and the hills are moderate, making it easy to add miles or to create your own favorite loop.

KEEP IN MIND

Although traffic is rarely heavy, some of the cars that do use this road seem to have a real issue abiding by the speed limit. There are three stop signs along the route and many cars treat them as little more than optional yields.

NEARBY NOTABLES

For some authentic ethnic replenishment, head back to Buford Highway. The many Hispanic and Asian restaurants are plenty casual enough for post-workout attire.

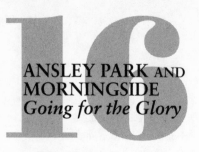

ANSLEY PARK AND MORNINGSIDE
Going for the Glory

DISTANCE
5.5 miles, 8.8 kilometers
(out and back)

HILL FACTOR
Significant

GETTING THERE
Approximately 3.5 miles northeast of downtown. Take I-75/85 to Tenth Street (exit 250), go east to Piedmont Avenue, turn left, and go to The Prado.

PARKING
Plenty of free, on-street parking is available on The Prado and the surrounding neighborhood streets. If you include a visit to the Atlanta Botanical Garden as part of your agenda, parking is included in the price of admission.

PUBLIC TRANSPORTATION
The area is located near the Arts Center MARTA Station and is served by the North Decatur (#36) bus, which departs from the Arts Center and Avondale Stations.

OVERVIEW
On Piedmont Avenue directly across from the midpoint of the Atlanta Botanical Garden is a road labeled The Prado. This juncture starts you on a jaunt through Ansley Park, Piedmont Heights, and Morningside, some of Atlanta's most beautiful and historic neighborhoods.

THE COURSE
MAIN ROUTE: This route begins at the intersection of Piedmont Avenue and The Prado, across the street from the Atlanta Botanical Garden. Take The Prado for almost 0.5 mile to Montgomery Ferry Road. You will see the junction for Montgomery Ferry just behind signs for Maddox Road to your right. Turn left on Montgomery Ferry and travel for 0.25 mile past the Ansley Golf Club. Montgomery Ferry repeatedly attempts to shake you off with unexpected turns, so keep an eye on the street signs. Continue for another 1.0 mile until Montgomery Ferry ends at Piedmont Avenue.

At Piedmont Avenue, turn left and go to the first traffic signal. Turn right on North Rock Springs Road and travel for almost 0.75 mile to the *second* North Pelham Road in-

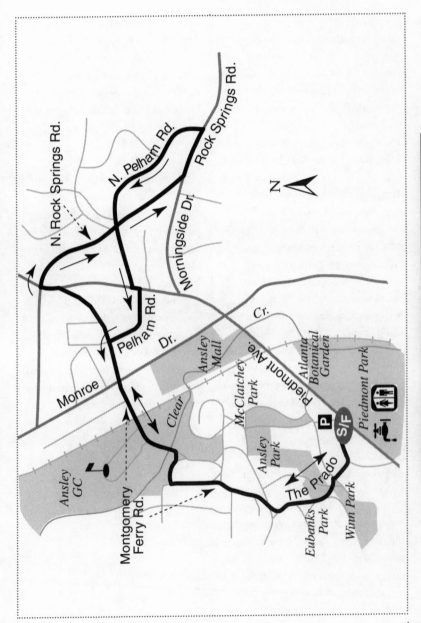

tersection. (Bypass the first, which occurs near the intersection of North Rock Springs Road and Piedmont Avenue at a traffic circle.) It may appear that you are on Morningside Drive, as these two roads merge for 0.25 mile. Your next turn is where Rock Springs Road and Morningside Drive diverge and numerous roads splinter off in multiple directions. From here, pick up North Pelham Road and follow it north for a little more than 1.0 mile to its intersection with Montgomery Ferry Road, crossing Rock Springs Road and Piedmont Avenue. Go straight through the traffic circle again. You may notice that the road has changed names from North Pelham to East Pelham to just plain Pelham Road. At Montgomery Ferry, turn left and retrace your steps back to your starting point just across from the Botanical Garden.

HIGHLIGHTS

The neighborhood roads are all wide and inviting, and almost always have sidewalks on at least one side of the road. There are many beautiful houses and landscapes. The Ansley Golf Club is also stunning. The bridge on Montgomery Ferry Road offers a magnif-

icent view of the Midtown skyline. Even though the roads sound confusing, this is an easy run to memorize. You can also plan a side trip to the Atlanta Botanical Garden or Piedmont Park. Many side streets make it easy to add miles.

KEEP IN MIND

Use caution whenever crossing Piedmont Avenue. Although there are traffic signals, these areas are usually very congested. Running on Ansley Golf Course cart paths is not allowed.

NEARBY NOTABLES

Piedmont Park has drinking fountains and grassy hills where you can relax and catch your breath. There are several food and beverage sources on Piedmont Road and at Ansley Mall.

VIRGINIA-HIGHLAND
High Times in the Highlands

DISTANCE
3.2 miles, 5.0 kilometers (loop)

HILL FACTOR
Moderate

GETTING THERE
Approximately 3.0 miles northeast of downtown. Take I-85 to North Druid Hills Road (exit 89) and go east to Briarcliff Road, then south to Johnson Road, which becomes North Highland Avenue.

PARKING
There is plenty of free parking on University Drive and other neighboring side streets off North Highland Avenue.

PUBLIC TRANSPORTATION
The area is served by the Noble (#16) MARTA bus, which departs from the Five Points Station.

OVERVIEW
Virginia-Highland, originally known as North Boulevard Park, is similar to many Atlanta communities that developed following the advent of the automobile. It suffered a significant decline following World War II when many residents moved to the suburbs. Now urban revitalization has made "the Highlands" one of Atlanta's favorite neighborhoods, filled with many quaint boutiques, charming houses, and a plethora of eateries. Of course, there is no better way to see almost everything this area has to offer than a leisurely run.

THE COURSE
MAIN ROUTE: Begin at the intersection of North Highland Avenue and University Drive. Go south on North Highland crossing Virginia Avenue. After a series of challenging hills, the route flattens out considerably. Turn left on St. Charles Avenue at the Hand in Hand pub. Although there is a sidewalk on St. Charles, it is hardly necessary. It's completely residential, the speed limit is 25, and there are plenty of speed bumps. At Briarcliff, turn left and go to Virginia Avenue. Make another left and go to North Virginia Avenue, where there's a traffic circle. Take North Virginia to Lanier Boulevard. Although these final transitions may sound a bit confusing, they are actually pretty

VIRGINIA-HIGHLAND

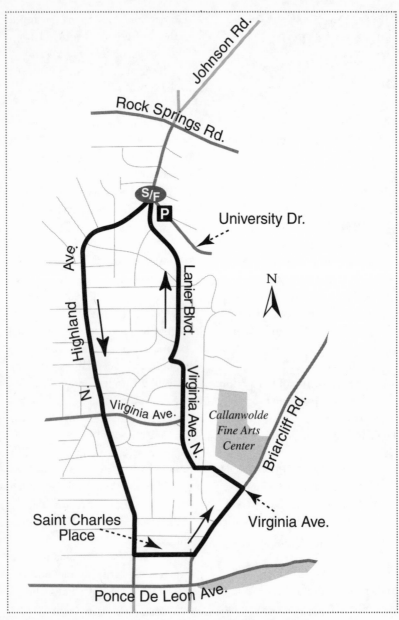

Johnson Rd.

Rock Springs Rd.

S/F

P

University Dr.

N

Ave.

Lanier Blvd.

Highland

Virginia Ave. N.

N.

Virginia Ave.

Callanwolde
Fine Arts
Center

Briarcliff Rd.

Saint Charles
Place

Virginia Ave.

Ponce De Leon Ave.

easy if you pay attention to the street signs. Take a right on Lanier, which ends near the intersection of University Drive and North Highland Avenue, where you began.

HIGHLIGHTS

This is an area that every Atlanta resident or visitor should get to know—and this run will help you do so. Sidewalks are available for the entire route. The section south of Virginia is home to Atkins Park Restaurant, the oldest restaurant in Atlanta, open since 1922. That says something in the restaurant industry!

KEEP IN MIND

In some places, the sidewalk is in less than perfect condition.

NEARBY NOTABLES

Atkins Park Restaurant is a good filling station. Or if your running takes you out early on a Saturday or Sunday morning, join the coffee-sipping crowd waiting for breakfast tables at Murphy's Restaurant. If Pabst Blue Ribbon is your post-run drink of choice, Moe's and Joe's Bar & Grill is your place.

18

THE FREEDOM PARKWAY TRAIL
Five Little Miles Near Little Five Points

DISTANCE
5.0 miles, 8.0 kilometers
(out and back)

HILL FACTOR
Moderate

GETTING THERE
Approximately 2.5 miles east of downtown. Take I-75/85 to North Avenue/Georgia Tech (exit 249D) and go east to North Highland Avenue. Turn left and go one block to Ponce de Leon Avenue. Turn right and go to South Ponce de Leon Avenue.

PARKING
Parking is available on South Ponce de Leon Avenue and other nearby streets.

PUBLIC TRANSPORTATION
The area is served by the Ponce de Leon (#2) MARTA bus, which departs from the North Avenue, Decatur, and Avondale Stations.

OVERVIEW
This route begins where the PATH Foundation first poured concrete in 1995 for their initial nonmotorized vehicle path. Now, after eight years, PATH has constructed a network of trails in this area, which is only the beginning of an ambitious two-county in-town path system. This route passes by two public spaces dedicated to continuing the work of two twentieth century leaders: Martin Luther King Jr. and Jimmy Carter.

THE COURSE
MAIN ROUTE: This route begins at the intersection of Ponce de Leon Avenue and South Ponce de Leon Avenue. Follow the path's main artery west from South Ponce de Leon Avenue toward downtown. The skyline will be visible by the end of mile 1.0. At the end of the trail, near the Martin Luther King Jr. National Historic Site, go north on Jackson Street, and follow the PATH signs on the sidewalk. Go west on Highland Avenue for approximately 0.5 mile to Piedmont Avenue. Although it's possible to continue into downtown, this is an appropriate place to turn around because the idyllic, traffic-free conditions deteriorate

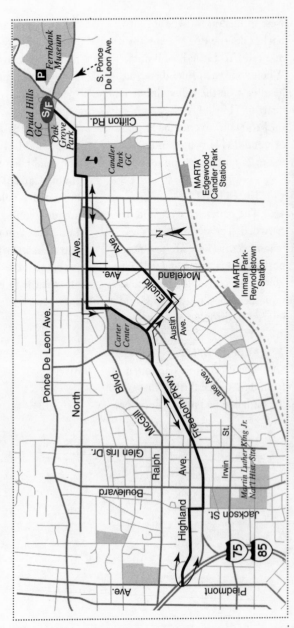

west of Piedmont. About halfway back, take the PATH extension marked "To Little Five Points." When you reach Euclid Avenue, head east on the sidewalk into the heart of "Little Five," then north on Moreland Avenue back to the original PATH route, and east to the original starting point.

HIGHLIGHTS

The paths are wide and never crowded. The skyline views are magnificent. There are few neighborhoods as unique as Little Five Points, which is filled with boutiques, eateries, music halls, and interesting people.

KEEP IN MIND

The PATH trails are open from dawn until dusk. The start of the path can be hard to find; look for nearby Moreland Avenue Baptist Church. In certain places, the main path twists and turns significantly; this is not the place for speed work.

NEARBY NOTABLES

The Martin Luther King Jr. National Historic Site and The Jimmy Carter Library and Museum are worth a field trip for you and any non-runners in your group. Little Five Points never ceases to entertain and offers many food and beverage establishments; casual attire is the rule of the day.

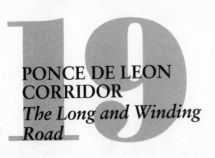

PONCE DE LEON CORRIDOR
The Long and Winding Road

DISTANCE
8.0 miles, 12.8 kilometers
(out and back)

HILL FACTOR
Moderate

GETTING THERE
Approximately 3.0 miles northeast of downtown. The western starting point is at the intersection of Moreland/Briarcliff and Ponce de Leon Avenues, 1.5 miles north of downtown. Take I-75/85 to North Avenue/Georgia Tech (exit 249D) and go east to Moreland Avenue, then north to Ponce de Leon.

The eastern starting point is at the intersection of Ponce de Leon Avenue and Sams Crossing, 7.0 miles east of downtown. Take I-285 to Ponce de Leon Avenue East (exit 40) and go west, to Sams Crossing.

PARKING
Parking is usually available at First United Methodist Church on Ponce de Leon Avenue east of Briarcliff or along the nearby side streets to the south, such as Fairview and Blue Ridge. Parking at the Avondale MARTA Station is for MARTA patrons only. Parking is permitted on Grove Avenue, east of Sams Crossing.

PUBLIC TRANSPORTATION
The eastern starting point is located near the Avondale MARTA Station. The western starting point is served by the Ponce de Leon (#2) bus, which departs from the North Avenue, Decatur, and Avondale Stations, and the Thomasville/ Lenox (#48) bus, which departs from the Lenox and Inman Park/ Reynoldstown Stations.

OVERVIEW
Ponce de Leon Avenue is one of Atlanta's longest streets. The middle portion takes you back in time more than any other street in the city. From Moreland Avenue/ Briarcliff Road to the Avondale MARTA Station, the road passes lovely houses, relatively unchanged in the last hundred years, as well as charming and historic downtown Decatur, incorporated in 1823, twenty-four years before Atlanta. There are wide sidewalks or foot-

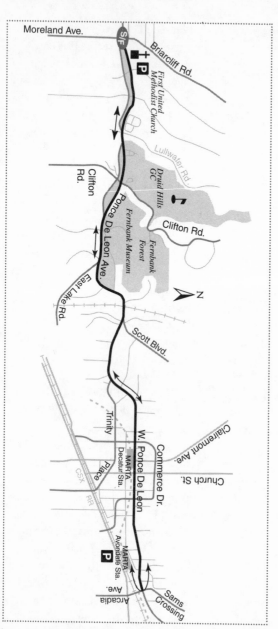

paths the entire way on both sides of the street.

THE COURSE

MAIN ROUTE: Ponce de Leon changes names twice during this route, to West Ponce de Leon Avenue, then East Ponce de Leon Avenue. Start at the offices of the Golden Key National Honor Society on Moreland Avenue and go east on Ponce de Leon Avenue. (Moreland also changes names to Briarcliff Road on the other side of the street.) The first mile is relatively flat, crossing Clifton Road and passing several different churches. Further along the way, you'll encounter two forks in the road. Keep left on Ponce at the first fork at East Lake Road. At the 2.0-mile mark, go under the old railroad bridge and take the right fork in the road; Ponce becomes West Ponce de Leon Avenue. The road gradually ascends for almost 1.0 mile as you enter the city of Decatur. A half mile later, you're at the other side of town and the street is now called East Ponce de Leon Avenue. The route ends 0.5 mile ahead at the intersection of Sams Crossing.

HIGHLIGHTS

Mature trees provide shade almost the entire way. The side streets, especially to the south, promise amazing architecture and beg you to add some distance and explore—just like the road's namesake did.

KEEP IN MIND

The sidewalks and footpaths are choppy in places. During rush hours on the west end of this route, traffic congestion—and the air pollution that comes with it—can make this run less pleasant.

NEARBY NOTABLES

There are a few convenience store/gas stations along Ponce for quick pick-ups. Downtown Decatur offers many places to stop for refreshment on or near Ponce de Leon. Several, such as The Brick Store Pub and Java Monkey Coffee have outside seating and a casual environment perfectly suited for runners.

PEACHTREE ROAD
Exploring the Big Peach

DISTANCE
11.0 miles, 17.6 kilometers
(one way)

HILL FACTOR
Significant

GETTING THERE
To reach the northern starting
point, approximately 10.5 miles
northeast of downtown, take I-285
to Ashford Dunwoody Road (exit
29), and go south to Peachtree Road.

PARKING
Parking is available along
Peachtree in retail lots after hours,
in commercial lots, or on side
streets. Some of the street parking
is metered.

PUBLIC TRANSPORTATION
There are several MARTA
stations on or near Peachtree, in-
cluding Chamblee, Brookhaven/
Oglethorpe University, Buckhead,
Lindbergh Center, Arts Center,
Civic Center, North Avenue,
Peachtree Center, Five Points, and
Garnett. The northern starting
point is served by the Peachtree
Industrial (#25) MARTA bus,
which departs from the Lenox Sta-
tion. The southern starting point
is three blocks from the Garnett
Station.

OVERVIEW
Peachtree Road is almost synonymous with running in Atlanta.
It hosts the world's largest 10K,
provides almost half the distance
for the Atlanta Marathon, and, as
the South's most famous thoroughfare, entertains hundreds of resident
and visiting runners everyday. Unfortunately, the growth of the city
of Atlanta has not been kind to the
running faithful. Increased traffic,
congestion, and construction are re-
sponsible for surroundings and
sidewalks that are less conducive to
safe passage than in times past.
Nonetheless, the natural beauty and
carefully planned layout of this
road continue to lure runners of all
abilities. Peachtree always delivers
a run that is scenic, exciting, and
challenging—and sure to bring you
back time and again.

Peachtree Road runs through
Brookhaven, Buckhead, Midtown,

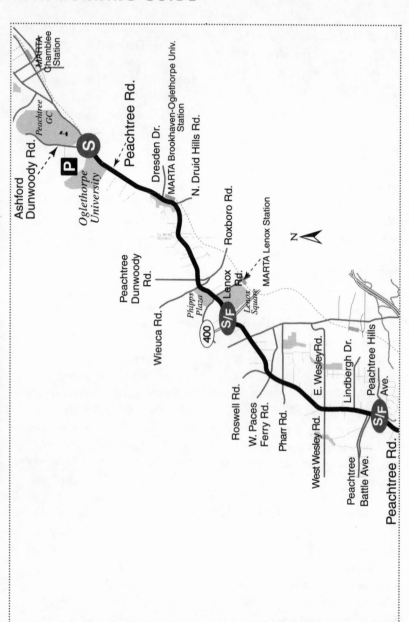

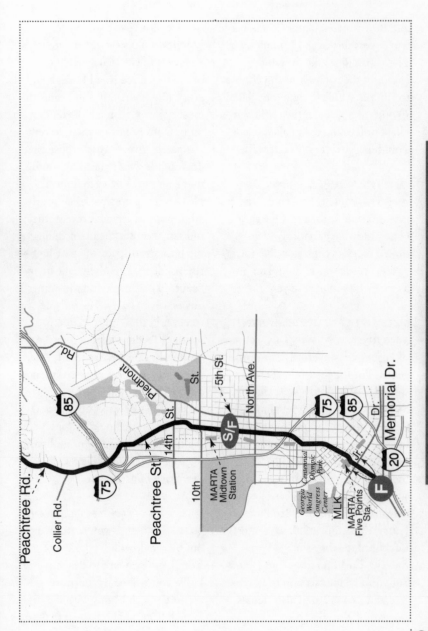

and downtown Atlanta. A one-way trip covers just over 11.0 miles. There are sidewalks the entire length of the route. You can choose to run the whole thing in one fell swoop, or approach the challenge like a time-starved Appalachian Trail hiker and do it in intervals.

THE COURSE

This route is broken down into 3.0-mile segments. Like the courses for the previously mentioned races, it begins on the north and proceeds south, but it can just as easily be run in reverse.

MILES 0.0–3.0: ASHFORD DUNWOODY ROAD TO LENOX SQUARE This section of Peachtree is relatively flat or rolls gently. For the first mile, there is a sidewalk only on the west side of the road. You get a brief glimpse of the downtown and midtown skylines as you pass Oglethorpe University, Brookhaven Park, and the Brookhaven/Oglethorpe University MARTA Station, opposite the entrance into Historic Brookhaven (entry 12). At mile 2.0, you enter Buckhead, passing Phipps Plaza, the Ritz-Carlton Hotel, and Lenox Square. The intersection of Peachtree and Lenox Road also signals the end of your first 5K.

MILES 3.1–6.0: LENOX SQUARE TO PEACHTREE HILLS AVENUE Lenox Square is the official starting point of the Peachtree Road Race, held every July Fourth. It also begins the most enjoyable stretch of running on Peachtree, as a gradual descent ultimately gives way to a blistering downhill (if you're heading south, that is; it may not seem quite as pleasant on a northward jaunt). In addition, this segment reveals the full scope of Buckhead, including the business district, the new high-rise residential buildings, the many beautiful churches, and the numerous places to party. The only detraction in this entire section is south of Piedmont from mile 3.5 until mile 4.5 at Pharr Road, where the traffic is more congested than at any other place on Peachtree. Although the sidewalks are in good shape, be on the lookout for emerging traffic at intersections and parking lots. You reach mile 6.0 at Peachtree Hills Avenue.

MILES 6.1–9.0: PEACHTREE HILLS AVENUE TO FIFTH STREET If you're not worn out by the downhill pilgrimage from Lenox Square to Peachtree Hills, you will be by this next section, which begins with the famed "Cardiac Hill"—more than

0.5 mile of significant ascent concluding at Piedmont Hospital. The good times continue to roll after you cross the bridge into Midtown on a gentle but seemingly never-ending ascent, passing the Woodruff Arts Center and the High Museum of Art. Downtown begins at mile 8.5 on Tenth Street, where you see the new Federal Reserve Building and the historic Margaret Mitchell House. This part of the journey concludes at Fifth Street near Cornerstone Village lofts.

MILES 9.1–11.3: FIFTH STREET TO MEMORIAL DRIVE Peachtree concludes in spectacular fashion for both the runner and the sightseer. The route passes the fabulous Fox Theater; the beautifully restored Georgian Terrace, known as "The Grand Old Lady of Peachtree;" the Bank of America Plaza, the tallest building in the south; and Crawford Long Hospital. At the 10.0-mile mark, you reach the heart of downtown, home to skyscrapers, retail stores, theme restaurants, luxury hotels, and, most importantly, wide sidewalks. Although the pedestrian traffic is heavy, problem-free passage is assured at even the busiest of times with a little courtesy. Around 10.5 miles, you encounter

Woodruff Park, Five Points (where the compass starts for Atlanta's street numbering), and Underground Atlanta. Although there are many street vendors and homeless people, the atmosphere is as inviting—and stimulating—as the downhill slope. For the last 0.5 mile south of Five Points, the condition of the storefronts and sidewalk deteriorates. At the intersection of Martin Luther King Jr. Drive, you hit mile 11.0; Peachtree ends shortly thereafter at Memorial Drive. If you've been running down Peachtree for the wrong reasons, you will discover another landmark—the Atlanta City Detention Center.

HIGHLIGHTS

There are too many highlights to mention all of them. Some are listed in the separate segments of the course. You'll pass through many of Atlanta's in-town neighborhoods, each with unique characteristics. Many unusual boutiques and bistros in their commercial centers are worthy of investigation.

KEEP IN MIND

Many vehicles pass uncomfortably close to runners. Drivers don't always pay attention and

some don't seem to know that
pedestrians have the right of way.

NEARBY NOTABLES

There are many places to buy
or beg water during your run and
purchase liquid refreshment after-
ward. Many offer al fresco drinking
and dining, where your running attire will fit in. Several establishments are also open late, which
may accommodate your running
schedule. Be aware, however, that
almost nothing may be open on
Sunday morning, though it's an excellent time to take advantage of
decreased traffic.

*Woodruff
Park in
downtown
Atlanta*

PIEDMONT PARK/ MIDTOWN
Where the Action Is

DISTANCE
1.5 to 2.5 miles,
2.4 to 4.0 kilometers (loop)
*(Does not include
Piedmont Park miles)*

HILL FACTOR
Slight

GETTING THERE
Approximately 3.0 miles
north of downtown. Take I-75/85
to Tenth Street (exit 250), and go
east to Piedmont Park.

PARKING
Free parking is available on
the south side of Tenth Street, but
can be challenging to find in the
evenings. Parking is permitted on
either side of Charles Allen Drive
and other neighborhood streets.
There are parking lots on Tenth
Street near the Grady High School
stadium; they are available and free
of charge sometimes but often
reserved for park events.

PUBLIC TRANSPORTATION
The area is located near the
Midtown MARTA Station and is
served by the North Decatur (#36)
bus, which departs from the Arts
Center and Avondale Stations.

OVERVIEW
Since 1887, Piedmont Park
has been Atlanta's most celebrated
playground. It is the site of the finish line of the Peachtree Road Race
as well as a number of cultural
events throughout the year. Runners and walkers use the park every
day, as do cyclists, rollerbladers,
Frisbee enthusiasts, and softball
and flag-football players. The
Midtown neighborhood offers
opportunities for park runners to
add variety and distance on the
safe, pleasant, and historic streets.

THE COURSE
There are many ways to enjoy
Piedmont Park as a runner. The wide
paths and roads make it easy to run
anywhere from 1.5 to 3.5 miles
without ever leaving the park. Most
of the interior paths are flat and
smooth, except for the steep asphalt
path leading up Oak Hill along
Tenth Street. Although the most
popular loop in the park encircles
the recreation fields and Lake Clara

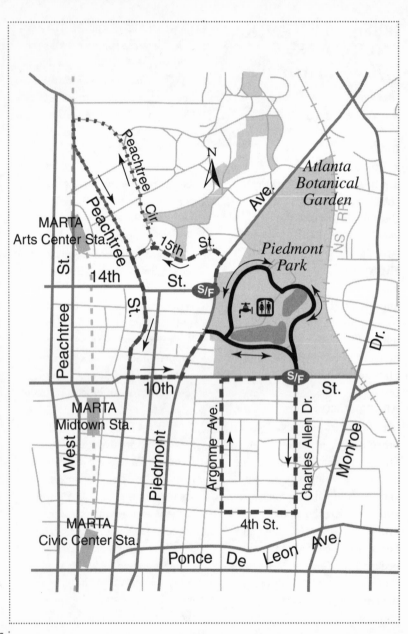

Meer, covering 3.0 miles, many runners carve out their own favorite routes. You won't be alone if your approach is to just run the interior roads until your watch or your body suggests that you've had enough.

If you want to test out some of the neighborhood roads, the options are equally unrestricted. Here are some popular and easy options:

FROM THE WEST AT PIEDMONT AND FOURTEENTH STREET — 1.25 MILES
Exit the park's main gate on Piedmont Avenue at Fourteenth Street, and cross to the other side of the road. Go north to Fifteenth Street (closed to incoming vehicular traffic), and turn left, passing historic Habersham Memorial Hall and the beautiful houses of Ansley Park. After little more than 0.5 mile, turn left on Peachtree Street. After another 0.5 mile, turn left on Tenth Street to return to the park.

FROM THE WEST AT PIEDMONT AND FOURTEENTH STREET — 2.5 MILES
From Fifteenth Street, turn right on Peachtree Circle, which has a wide pedestrian/cyclist lane. Turn left on Peachtree Street and return to the park.

FROM THE SOUTH AT TENTH STREET AND CHARLES ALLEN DRIVE — 1.25 MILES
Exit the park on Charles Allen Drive. Turn right on Fourth Street and run up a formidable hill. Turn right again on Argonne Avenue and return to the park. Fortunately, traffic on Argonne is almost always light enough for you to take to the street, avoiding the dilapidated sidewalks.

HIGHLIGHTS

No motorized travel is permitted inside the park. There are spots throughout the park where you can rest or the non-runners in your group can wait. Grady High School, across from the park's southeast corner, has a regulation-sized track that is open occasionally for those wanting to run laps.

KEEP IN MIND

The park is popular with dog walkers and parents with young children. Also pay attention to the cyclists and rollerbladers on the paths. The sidewalks on Tenth Street between Peachtree Street and Piedmont Park are often congested.

NEARBY NOTABLES

The Park Tavern, Arden's Garden, Mellow Mushroom Pizza Bakers, and Fabiano's Italian Deli are all located near the intersection of Tenth Street and Monroe Drive. The Prince of Wales pub, across the street from the park's main gates on Piedmont, is a perfect place to liquid carbo-load. The Atlanta Botanical Garden, next door to the park, is a great diversion before, after, or separate from your run. (An admission fee is required.)

Piedmont Park

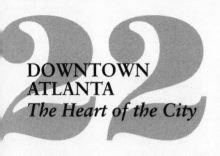

DOWNTOWN ATLANTA
The Heart of the City

DISTANCE
5.0 miles, 8.0 kilometers (loop)

HILL FACTOR
Moderate

GETTING THERE
From the south, take I-75/85 north to Andrew Young International Boulevard (exit 248C), and go west to Centennial Olympic Park.

From the north, take I-75/85 south to North Avenue (exit 249D), and go east on North Avenue. Turn south on Spring Street (name changes to Centennial Olympic Park Drive) to Centennial Olympic Park.

PARKING
It can be challenging to find free parking during the workday. On weekdays, some two-hour, non-metered parking is available across the street from Centennial Olympic Park on Nassau, Luckie, and Walton Streets, as well as on the east side of Centennial Olympic Park Way about 0.5 mile north of the park. In the evenings and on weekends, there are more places available for free parking without time restrictions. Campus parking at Georgia Tech and Georgia State is by permit only.

PUBLIC TRANSPORTATION
The park is across the street from the Dome/Georgia World Congress Center/Philips Arena/CNN Center MARTA Station.

OVERVIEW
Centennial Olympic Park, a legacy from Atlanta's 1996 Olympics, is the centerpiece of urban revitalization in downtown Atlanta. Nearby, old architecture mixes with the new of Georgia State University's expansion in the area. Atlanta sits at a higher elevation above sea level than almost any other American metropolis. This becomes more apparent as you launch your run at the city center.

THE COURSE
MAIN ROUTE: Although this run can be started anywhere along the route, Centennial Olympic Park is an ideal location for a pre-run stretching session or a post-run cool down. From here, go north on Centennial Olympic Park Way, away

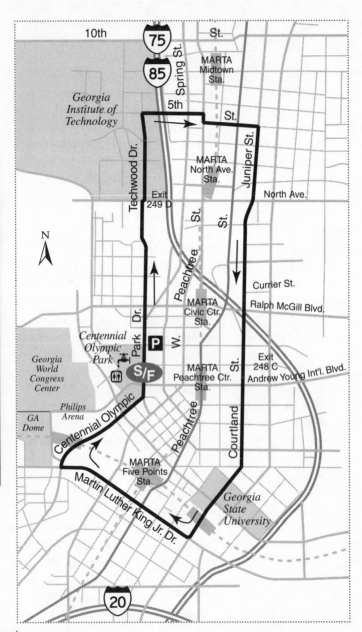

from the park and through Centennial Place. This subsidized housing complex, almost 0.5 mile from the park, is another Olympic legacy and has become a model for similar programs across the country. At North Avenue, the street changes names to Techwood Drive and heads into the Georgia Institute of Technology campus and passes Bobby Dodd Stadium at Grant Field, site of the most lopsided game in college football history. In 1916, Georgia Tech beat Cumberland College 222–0. Continue on Techwood Drive, past campus organizations and fraternity houses. Turn right on Fifth Street, at the Phi Kappa Sigma house 0.5 mile past the stadium.

Fifth Street, lined by a pedestrian/cyclist lane, takes a brief jog at the intersection of West Peachtree Street. Turn right and then left again back onto Fifth, just south of the Biltmore Hotel. At 1.0 mile into your run, turn right on Juniper Street. At the Third Street intersection there is an historical marker noting the site of the 1862 execution of James J. Andrews, Union spy and train thief (as depicted in the movie called *The Great Locomotive Chase*). Shortly after this historical marker, Juniper changes name to Courtland Street.

Follow Courtland Street on an uphill climb into the downtown hotel district. Pass by the Martin Luther King Jr. National Historic Site, cross Auburn Avenue (site of King's birth), and through Georgia State University. After 4.0 miles, turn right on Martin Luther King Jr. Drive, across from the Georgia State Capitol. Take MLK Drive 0.5 mile to Centennial Olympic Park Way. Turn right again and head back to the park. This part of the route, over some of Atlanta's original train yards, reveals the downtown skyline and the Georgia Dome and Philips Arena, homes of the Atlanta Falcons, Hawks, and Thrashers.

HIGHLIGHTS

This tour is a great way to see the home bases of some of Atlanta's heaviest corporate hitters, including CNN, Turner Broadcasting, Georgia Power, *The Atlanta Journal-Constitution*, BellSouth, and Coca-Cola. In fact, Coca-Cola fans, this route passes Coca-Cola World Headquarters, the original Coca-Cola Bottling Company (125 Edgewood Avenue, now the Georgia

State University Baptist Student
Union), and the World of Coca-
Cola at Underground Atlanta. On a
hot, summer day, follow Atlanta's
youth into the fountains in Centennial Olympic Park.

KEEP IN MIND

The intersection of Centennial
Olympic Park Way and West Peachtree Street can be a tricky crossing;
exercise caution and use the crosswalks. The two blocks on Courtland,
around Currier Street and Ralph
McGill Boulevard, can become a bit
questionable later in the evening. It is
always wise to confine evening running to well-lit public areas where
other people are present.

NEARBY NOTABLES

There are too many resources
for food and beverage to list them
all. Drinks and hot dogs are available at the information center in
the park. Both CNN Center, across
the street, and Underground Atlanta, at Marietta and Pryor Streets,
have food courts. Dania Gourmet, a
small take-out deli and grocery
store at the corner of Marietta and
Peachtree, offers water and cold
drinks as well as prepared meals to
go. Runners in their workout attire
are welcome in all these venues.

Centennial Olympic Park

Glover Park

on the square

in Marietta

AROUND ATLANTA

THE SILVER COMET TRAIL
Runnin' the Rails

DISTANCE
25.6 miles, 41.0 kilometers (out and back)
See Alternates, below, for full trail distance

HILL FACTOR
Nonexistent

GETTING THERE
Approximately 15 miles northwest of downtown. Take I-285 to South Cobb Drive/GA 280 (exit 15), and go west to Cooper Lake Road, west to Mavell Road, then south to the Silver Comet trailhead.

PARKING
Free parking is available at the trailhead. On spring and summer weekends, overflow parking is located at the Nickajack Elementary School, just 0.1 mile from the main lot.

OVERVIEW
Atlanta has long been criticized for a lack of pedestrian and bike paths. Sidewalks, bicycle lanes, and multi-recreational trails historically have occurred to planners after the fact. Today, however, an evolution is taking place that promises to change the landscape for local runners, cyclists, walkers, rollerbladers, and hikers as well. The PATH Foundation (entries 7 and 14) is working diligently with city governments, civic groups, and concerned citizens throughout the metropolitan area to ensure and promote increased opportunities for safe recreation and pollution-free transportation. Nowhere is the hard work more evident than on the Silver Comet Trail.

The Silver Comet Trail is Georgia's most ambitious "rails to trails" project—railroad routes that have been converted to recreation trails. The Trail takes its name from a train that traveled through the area from 1947 to 1968. Originating in Boston, the *Silver Comet* would make its way through Atlanta to Birmingham, Alabama. Today this trail follows the same route, from Atlanta toward the Alabama state line (and beyond, on Alabama's Chief Ladiga Trail). Much of the work—37.6 miles of the proposed 57-mile route—is already finished and in use.

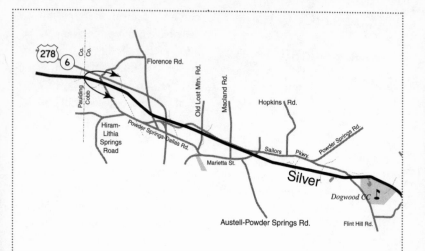

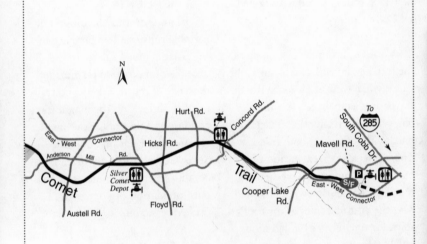

THE COURSE

The Silver Comet Trail begins in Smyrna in Cobb County and passes through Paulding and Polk counties. This entry focuses on the first 12.8 miles of trail maintained by Cobb County.

MAIN ROUTE: From the beginning of the trail at Mavell Road to the Cobb County line west of Florence Road, the path is asphalt, ten feet wide, flat, relatively straight, and usually lined with foliage on both sides. This route is a perfect location for marathon training. On weekends the path can be somewhat crowded near the visitors center at the trail's start. Fortunately, any congestion quickly dissipates as you make your way west. The farther west you travel, the more remote the surroundings become. Additional trailheads along the way are ideal places to get water or use the rest room. Regular mile markers ensure that you cover the distance you desire.

ALTERNATE: The entire trail is just over 37 miles. There are thirteen different trailheads throughout the three-county area accessible by vehicle, so you can customize a running route that is as long, variable, and as peaceful as you like. Check the complete Silver Comet Trail map available at the depot at Floyd Road or on their website (see below) for further details.

HIGHLIGHTS

This is among the most comfortable runs you'll experience in the Atlanta area because of the absence of motorized traffic, the presence of mile markers and trailhead facilities, and the magnificent condition of the trail. Continuously updated information about all Silver Comet trail activities and conditions can be found at: www. pathfoundation.org or www. trailexpress.com.

KEEP IN MIND

Even though there are abundant trailside reminders to "stay on the right, pass on the left" and a center line running the length of the course, the occasional maniac reminds you that it makes sense to keep your eyes open. Despite the constant presence of greenery and trees on the side of the path, much of the trail is void of overhead cover. Combined with the heat from the asphalt surface and Atlanta's typical summer weather, the conditions can be very warm.

NEARBY NOTABLES

Rest rooms, water, and pay phones are available at several trailheads along the way. Snack foods and drinks may be purchased at the Silver Comet Depot located at the Floyd Road intersection (mile marker 4.2). There's also a convenience store adjacent to the Silver Comet Depot. Other food outlets are available at many of the major intersections on the routes to the trailheads.

MARIETTA
A Run That's Right on Track

DISTANCE
5.0 miles, 8.0 kilometers (loop)

HILL FACTOR
Mild

GETTING THERE
Approximately 16 miles northwest of downtown. Take I-75 north to Marietta Parkway/GA 120 (exit 263) and go west to Powder Springs Street, then north to Whitlock Road, then east to the Marietta Square.

PARKING
Plenty of metered parking is available around the Square. Parking is free on weekends and in the evenings.

PUBLIC TRANSPORTATION
The area is served by the #15, #40, and #45 Cobb County Transit (CCT) buses. CCT connects with MARTA at the Arts Center Station.

OVERVIEW
Marietta is one of Atlanta's better-known suburbs. Just like Atlanta, it developed as a hub for the early railroad system in the South and was an important site during the Civil War. These two themes came together in especially dramatic fashion in early 1862 when Federal raiders hijacked the locomotive *General* from the Marietta train depot. The pursuit that ensued was recreated almost a century later in Walt Disney's *The Great Locomotive Chase*. This route crosses those same infamous railroad tracks four times.

THE COURSE
MAIN ROUTE: Start on Church Street at the Marietta Square, home to a park, a beautiful fountain, and an old-time bandstand and gazebo. Head north on the brick-covered sidewalk past a number of shops, some of which have been in business for generations. After 0.5 mile, turn left on Kennesaw Avenue. The first railroad crossing is on this street. After another 0.5 mile, turn right on Sessions Street and cross the tracks again. Kennesaw Mountain can be seen in the distance to the right.

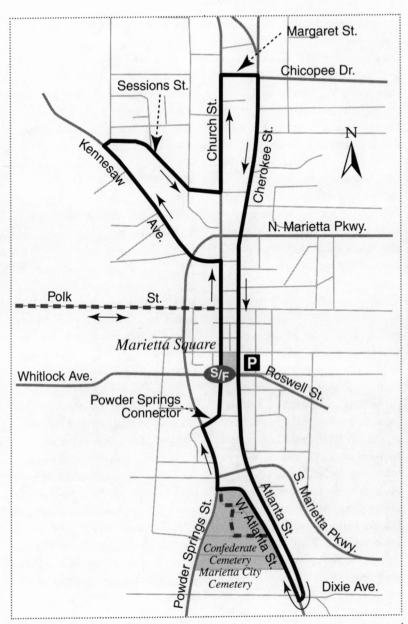

Margaret St.

Chicopee Dr.

Sessions St.

Church St.

Cherokee St.

N

Kennesaw

Ave.

N. Marietta Pkwy.

Polk   St.

Marietta Square

S/F

P

Roswell St.

Whitlock Ave.

Powder Springs
Connector

Powder Springs St.

W. Atlanta St.

Atlanta St.

S. Marietta Pkwy.

*Confederate
Cemetery
Marietta City
Cemetery*

Dixie Ave.

MARIETTA

Sessions Street ends back at Church Street. Turn left, go to Margaret Street and turn right. Follow Margaret Street to Cherokee Street, turn right, and run 2.0 miles back through the town square. Cherokee Street becomes Atlanta Street on the other side of the square. Follow Atlanta Street past Marietta Parkway, and up the only hill of any significance on this route. Turn right on Dixie Street (the first place to turn right), cross over the railroad tracks, and once again head north, this time on West Atlanta Street.

On West Atlanta Street, you'll pass the Confederate Cemetery, the final resting place for many Southern soldiers who perished in the Battle of Chickamauga in 1863. If you wish to run through the cemetery, use the second entrance; 0.25 mile later, the road deposits you at the northeast exit. To avoid the cemetery option, simply stay on West Atlanta; the road wraps around the grounds to the same exit, which brings you to a pedestrian path to Powder Springs Road. Turn right on Powder Springs Road and cross over Marietta Parkway. Take the next right, Powder Springs Connector, and go back across the railroad tracks to Church Street. Go north

on Church Street for 0.5 mile back to the Square.

ALTERNATE: Most of the nearby roads have sidewalks and are worth adding to your run. Polk Street, which has many restored Victorian houses, is of particular interest.

HIGHLIGHTS
Architecture fans will get their fill of old houses and businesses along the route.

KEEP IN MIND
The town square area can become congested with both automobiles and pedestrians. There are quite a few traffic lights along the route so be sure to use pedestrian crossing signals.

NEARBY NOTABLES
No trip to Marietta is complete without a visit to the many shops and restaurants in the historic town square. Runners with a serious hunger may try the Marietta Pizza Company or La Famiglia, a family-owned Italian restaurant. To quench a thirst, try Hemingway's Tropical Bar & Grill. Sarah Jean's Old Fashioned Ice Cream provides frozen treats.

EAST COBB
Shootin' the 'Hooch on Foot

DISTANCE
5.0 miles, 8.0 kilometers
(out and back)

HILL FACTOR
Nonexistent

GETTING THERE
Approximately 14 miles northwest of downtown Atlanta. Take I-285 to Riverside Drive (exit 24) and go north to Johnson Ferry Road, then west to Columns Drive.

PARKING
Parking is available for $2.00 in the Chattahoochee River NRA lot at Columns Drive. An annual permit is available for $25.00. There are two other lots, with the same requirements, by the recreation fields near the intersection of Columns and Johnson Ferry.

PUBLIC TRANSPORTATION
The area is served by the #60 and #65 Cobb Country Transit (CCT) buses. The #60 bus departs from the Dunwoody MARTA Station.

OVERVIEW
Columns Drive connects the west side of the Cochran Shoals unit of the Chattahoochee River Recreation Area with Johnson Ferry Road. A magnificent pedestrian/cyclist lane runs the entire way. The route also features marvelous architecture, golf course views, and interesting terrain. It's easy to see why this is one of the most popular roads to run in metropolitan Atlanta.

THE COURSE
MAIN ROUTE: This route travels northeast on Columns Drive to Johnson Ferry Road. The first mile is lined with luxury townhouse developments and views of the Chattahoochee River. The names of the subdivision tell you how close you are to the river: River Plantation, Riverview, River Place, and River Heights, to name a few. During the second mile, you pass the Atlanta Country Club and dozens of lovely houses. The final 0.5 mile is a stunning combination of bluffs to the left and wetlands to the right. The only traffic signal is located at the end of Columns Drive, telling you to turn around and take it in all over again.

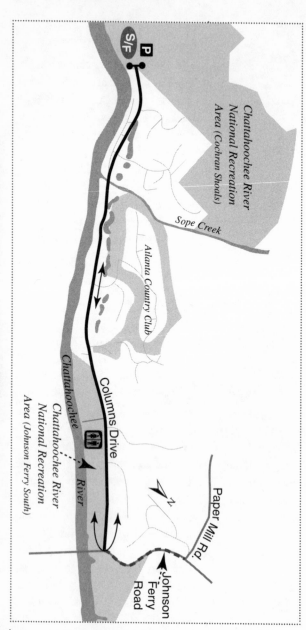

ALTERNATE: If you become bored with the relatively flat terrain of this route, turn left on Johnson Ferry Road. Take the sidewalk for 0.5 mile up—actually, up, up, up—to Paper Mill Road.

This is also the perfect place to blend road and trail running. Two separate units of the Chattahoochee River National Recreation Area (entry 38) are within sight of either end of Columns Drive. The southwest corner of Columns Drive is also the trailhead for the Cochran Shoals unit, and the Johnson Ferry North unit is across the street on the other side of Johnson Ferry Road.

HIGHLIGHTS
The pedestrian/cyclist lanes are wide and well marked. Regular visits to Columns Drive will acquaint you with the area's growth as plans for many more showy East Cobb homes are underway. Portable toilets are available at two different parking areas on the west side of Columns Drive within 1.0 mile of the Johnson Ferry intersection.

KEEP IN MIND
"Share the road" is a phrase often used by cyclists. On Columns Drive, it applies to runners as well as automobiles, as the designated lane receives significant bicycle traffic at peak times.

NEARBY NOTABLES
Plenty of fuel centers to grab a cold drink and fast food are located north on Johnson Ferry Road, past Paper Mill Road. You'll also find a couple of casual dining spots here.

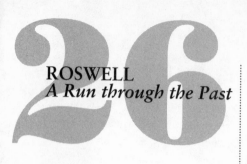

ROSWELL
A Run through the Past

DISTANCE
6.0 or 11.5 miles,
9.6 or 18.4 kilometers
(out and back)

HILL FACTOR
Mild (Slight) or Extreme

GETTING THERE
Approximately 21 miles north of downtown. From I-285, take GA 400 (exit 27) to Northridge Road (exit 6) and go west to Roswell Road, then north to Azalea Drive. Turn left and go to Willeo Road, then turn left again and go to the Riverside parking lot on the south side of the road, just west of the Fulton-Cobb County line.

PARKING
There is plenty of free parking at the starting point. Additional parking is available along Azalea Drive and at the Roswell River Landing.

PUBLIC TRANSPORTATION
The area is served by the Roswell/Alpharetta (#85) MARTA bus, which departs from the North Springs MARTA Station.

OVERVIEW
Oh, if only all suburbia had a place as well suited for runners as this multiuse roadway along the Chattahoochee River Park. Spacious pedestrian/cyclist lanes, even pavement, and wide-open river views are just a few of the attractions in the first part of this route. In the second portion, get ready for historical sites, splendid architecture, and a charming retail and entertainment district. You'll pay a "steep" price to enjoy the second part, but it is well worth it.

THE COURSE
FOR 6.0 MILES Head northeast on Willeo Road along the waterway and wetlands, running against traffic. The water levels vary greatly depending on rainfall and dam activity, so the view is unpredictable but never disappointing. As you pass the Big Creek Water Reclamation Plant, rest assured that any unpleasant odor disappears within a quarter of a mile, before you reach the Chattahoochee Nature Center. A brief detour into the nature center and a loop on its woodland

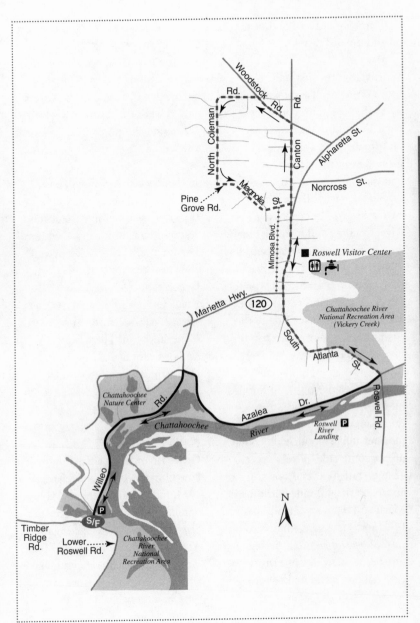

ROSWELL

trail, circling Beaver Pond, nets you an additional 1.5 miles.

Shortly after the first mile, turn south on Azalea Drive, well marked by traffic signals and prominent signage, and run in the pedestrian/cyclist lane. The 2.0-mile point is located near the park's picnic area and the playground. The final mile on Azalea, just as flat as the first two, takes you by the Roswell River Landing and historical markers detailing the importance of this section of the river during the Civil War. Upon your arrival at Atlanta Street, turn around and, for safety's sake, use the opposite side of the road to make your return trip for a total of 6.0 miles.

FOR 11.5 MILES If you're up for almost twice the distance, turn left on Atlanta Street and climb the monster hill. The sidewalk is only on the south side of the street. Things start to level off as you approach the 4.0-mile mark near Marietta Highway, the old Roswell Mill, and some scenic bluffs to the east. Shortly thereafter, the signature brick sidewalks of historic Roswell begin and you pass the Roswell Visitors Center.

At 4.5 miles, cross Magnolia Street. Atlanta Street changes name to Canton Road. Do not follow the signs directing traffic to Georgia Highways 120 and 9. If you are not into the heart of historic Roswell soon after this point, you've gone the wrong way.

In the city center, you will pass galleries, antique stores, and boutiques, as well as some beautifully restored bungalows and Victorian homes. Where the brick sidewalk ends near the aptly named Corner Grocery, turn left on Woodstock Road and head downhill. As the street levels out, turn left on North Coleman Road. There is no stop sign or traffic signal here, but it's the first place you can turn left. You'll spot a wide pedestrian/cyclist lane.

North Coleman Road ends at Pine Grove Road. Turn left again on Pine Grove Road (which changes name to Magnolia Street) and head uphill. Fortunately, the ascent is brief and you arrive, once again, at Atlanta Street/Canton Road. Turn right on Atlanta Street and make your way back to Azalea Drive and the Chattahoochee River Park.

ALTERNATE: Should you wish to see more of Roswell, turn right from Pine Grove Road onto Mimosa Boulevard before you get to Atlanta Street/Canton Road. You pass Primrose Cottage, which alone will make this detour worthwhile. Go east on any of the roads running perpendicular to Mimosa Boulevard or run through the Roswell Square to connect back to Atlanta Street.

HIGHLIGHTS

The pedestrian/cyclist lanes along the river are wide enough for two people to run side-by-side. There is plenty of picnic space and playground equipment at the Chattahoochee River Park to keep the non-runners in your party entertained. This run can easily be connected with the Vickery Creek unit of the Chattahoochee National Recreation Area (entry 38).

KEEP IN MIND

Though it is simple to incorporate the Chattahoochee Nature Center in your run, the hours—Monday–Saturday, 9:00 AM–5:00 PM; Sunday, 12:00 PM–5:00 PM—are somewhat restrictive. Admission is $3.00 for adults and $1.00 for children under age 12. Also, the majority of other users here are, in all likelihood, enjoying a more leisurely pace. The speed limit is rarely enforced on Willeo Road and Azalea Drive. For this reason, make sure to run against the direction of the vehicular traffic.

NEARBY NOTABLES

Downtown Roswell is always a pleasure to explore. If you are in need of a good carbohydrate load, Fratelli di Napoli Ristorante is always a hit. There are plenty of convenience stores west of the intersection of Azalea Drive and Atlanta Street where you can grab a bottled water, sports drink, or snack. On Wednesdays through Sundays during the summer, try to finish your run by 6:00 PM and take a guided canoe trip from the Chattahoochee Nature Center. Visit their website at www.chattnature center.com for more details.

27

ALPHARETTA
Blazing a Path along Big Creek

DISTANCE
12.0 miles, 19.2 kilometers
(out and back)

HILL FACTOR
Nonexistent

GETTING THERE
Approximately 16 miles northeast of downtown. Take I-285 to GA 400 North (exit 27) to Mansell Road (exit 8), and go east on Northpoint Parkway, then north to Big Creek Greenway.

PARKING
Plenty of free parking is available at the trailhead.

PUBLIC TRANSPORTATION
Northpoint Mall is served by the Mansell Road/Park-Ride (#140) MARTA bus, which departs from the North Springs Station.

OVERVIEW
Big Creek Greenway in Alpharetta is a recent and successful addition to the growing number of multiuse trails in the Atlanta area. It contains over 6.0 miles of pathways, showcasing the waterway namesake. Big Creek is located less than 1.0 mile from Northpoint Mall Atlanta in one of Georgia's fastest growing areas.

THE COURSE
MAIN ROUTE: This route begins in the Big Creek Greenway parking lot. From the trailhead, go 0.5 mile to the first pedestrian intersection. Proceed to the left at Location L-1 (noted on a sign) on the pathway located near a call box.

From here, it couldn't be easier to follow the wide, uninterrupted paved trail, which continues for another 5.5 miles, passing a variety of environmentally sensitive areas that contain an array of native trees and plants. You also may hear a cacophony of birds; over three dozen varieties have been sighted in the area. As you pass under the bridge for Old Alabama Road, you have reached the 1.5-mile mark. The crossing at Kimball Bridge Road marks the 3.0-mile point, and the Ed Isakson/Alpharetta Family YMCA parking lot is located at the 5.25-mile mark. The trail concludes just over 6.0 miles from the

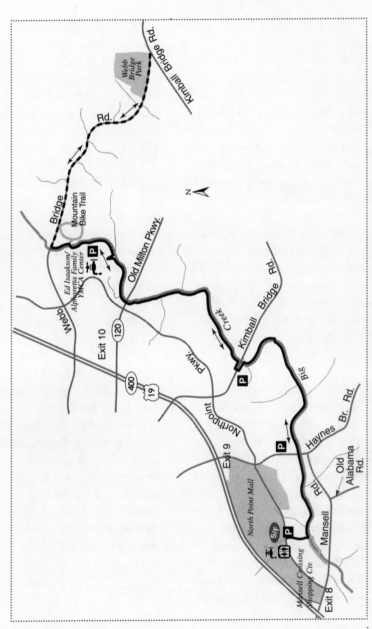

start at Webb Bridge Road.

ALTERNATE: If you wish to run additional miles, don't turn around at the Big Creek Greenway's northern terminus. Continue southeast on the wide sidewalk of Webb Bridge Road for another 2.0 miles until the road ends at Kimball Bridge Road. (The name changes to Webb Bridge *Way* for the final 0.5 mile.) For a slight variation, follow the signs to Webb Bridge Park at the intersection of Webb Bridge Road and Webb Bridge Way, where there's a post office. There is a hilly gravel path in the park that is 1.0 mile long and hosts the local schools' cross-country meets.

HIGHLIGHTS

This is a great option for a longer training run. Dense foliage in the summer keeps you in the shade most of the way. There is a well-maintained rest room at the trailhead and a portable toilet is located to the north of the trail's crossing at Kimball Bridge. Water fountains are available on the trail on the backside of the Ed Isakson/ Alpharetta Family YMCA and at the trailhead. Mileage markers are posted every 0.5 mile. Emergency

call boxes are located along the trail. It is not uncommon to see deer on the trails in the early morning hours, and gigantic hawks overhead later in the day. For those more interested in the area's shopping possibilities, Northpoint Mall Atlanta is minutes away.

KEEP IN MIND

Other trail users include walkers (with and without dogs and baby strollers), rollerbladers, and bicyclists. On weekends, there are many families on bikes. Significant efforts have been made to preserve this area, so please stay on the trails and do not disturb wildlife or plants.

NEARBY NOTABLES

Finding a place to refuel after a big day at Big Creek is as simple as following the trail. Mansell Crossing and Northpoint Mall, which both have entrances on Northpoint Parkway near the trailhead parking lot, offer casual and quick dining options. Adjacent to the mall, you'll find a number of chain restaurants, including Chili's and Cozymel's.

SANDY SPRINGS
Heading up the Hills

DISTANCE
6.0 miles, 9.6 kilometers (loop)

HILL FACTOR
Significant

GETTING THERE
Approximately 12 miles north of downtown. Take I-285 to Powers Ferry Road/Northside Drive/ New Northside Drive (exit 22) and go south to Powers Ferry Landing.

PARKING
Plenty of free parking is available at the Powers Ferry Landing shopping center and the Holiday Inn Crowne Plaza. Respect the hours posted on signs. If you wish to start this trek from another location along the way, parking is available on many side streets.

PUBLIC TRANSPORTATION
The area is served by the Powers Ferry (#148) MARTA bus which departs from the Sandy Springs Station.

OVERVIEW
Whether you face north or south when you're standing in the parking lot of the Powers Ferry Landing on Northside Drive, you'll come to the same conclusion: it is a long way up. Don't be intimidated by your valley vantage point. You're in the perfect spot to begin a challenging, yet rewarding pedestrian-friendly route in the heart of Sandy Springs.

THE COURSE
MAIN ROUTE: Although you can start in either direction, I recommend heading north on Northside Drive. This gets the busy I-285 intersection out of the way early. Both Northside and New Northside Drives cross the interstate; make sure to take Northside, so that you run against traffic. The first 1.5 miles don't have a sidewalk, but the road and the shoulder are both wide enough to accommodate runners safely. Northside Drive curves to the right and becomes Heards Ferry Road after 1.0 mile and the initial climb. Follow Heards Ferry for 2.0 miles up a series of hills (one of which is over 1.0 mile in length) and past some spectacular houses. After the intersection of

SANDY SPRINGS

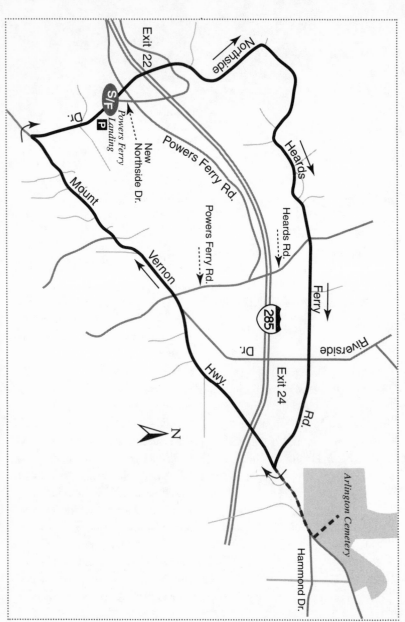

Heards Ferry Road and Heards Drive, the sidewalk ends on the south side of the road and begins on the north.

Heards Ferry Road ends at scenic Mount Vernon Highway. Turn right and run on the flat, wide, well-maintained sidewalk; there are fabulous views to the south, occasionally including downtown Atlanta. Follow Mount Vernon for 2.5 miles until it meets Northside Drive again. The last 0.5 mile on Mt. Vernon doesn't have a sidewalk, but fortunately the shoulder is more than adequate. Turn right on Northside and pick up the pedestrian/cyclist lane. Think about that imposing view back at the start—and rejoice because it's all downhill from here. At times, the road winds steeply downhill as it takes you 0.75 mile through rock outcroppings and underneath thick tree cover back to the Powers Ferry Landing.

ALTERNATE: It's easy to add miles by running 0.5 mile on Mt. Vernon Highway, east of the Heards Ferry intersection, to Arlington Cemetery. One of the city's largest graveyards, its roads are wide and well groomed, and the area is understandably quiet.

HIGHLIGHTS
Plenty of tree cover keeps you hidden from the sun on much of this route. Where there are sidewalks, they are in perfect condition.

KEEP IN MIND
If your departure is from the Holiday Inn Crown Plaza, make sure that you are on Northside Drive, not New Northside Drive. The pedestrian/cyclist lane on the east side of Northside Drive south of I-285 is a bit narrow in places as a result of fallen tree branches and debris—yet another reason for you to run in the suggested clockwise direction.

NEARBY NOTABLES
The Powers Ferry Village has a number of options for a casual meal or a grab 'n' go beverage or snack. Rest rooms are available at the many gas stations and fast-food restaurants nearby.

LILBURN
A Run Back in Time

DISTANCE
6.0 miles, 10.0 kilometers
(out and back)

HILL FACTOR
Moderate

GETTING THERE
Approximately 18 miles northeast of downtown. Take I-85 north to Indian Trail Lilburn Road (exit 101) and go south to Lawrenceville Highway/US-29/GA 8. Turn right, then left on Main Street to Lilburn City Park.

PARKING
The Lilburn City Park is at the starting point and has plenty of free parking. The Calvin Fitchett Municipal Complex, adjacent to the park, has additional space should the park's lot be full.

OVERVIEW
The small community of Lilburn is part of Gwinnett County, among the fastest growing counties in the United States. It has struggled to determine whether it wants to be part of the surrounding dense development, or fight the encroaching progress and maintain its independence from suburban Atlanta. At almost every turn, residential preservation efforts confront local growth initiatives. Camp Creek Road is a good indication of this conflict. Rural scenery and rustic charm abut recently completed subdivisions. With three schools, three churches, and a sidewalk every step of the way, Camp Creek Road is Atlanta's corridor of contrasts.

THE COURSE
MAIN ROUTE: Begin at the Lilburn City Park, where Main Street becomes Camp Creek Road, just down the hill from the quaint downtown. Heading southeast on the sidewalk, ascend the first of many hills. After the first mile you'll cross a footbridge. At 2.0 miles, cross busy Arcado Road, marked with traffic signals and a crosswalk. This is the only place on the route where you need to have your wits about you, as cross traffic is steady and often going faster than the speed limit. Camp Creek Road becomes Cole Drive just south of Arcado Road. Turn around less than

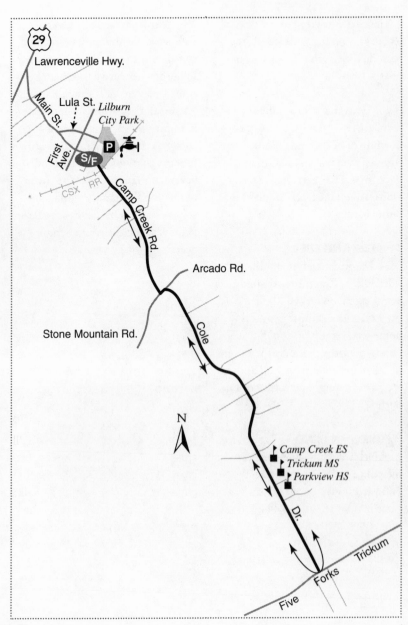

1.0 mile later at Five Forks Trickum Road. Stay on the same side of the road on the return trip so you can use the sidewalk.

If you want to attain a full 6.0 miles, there are two options. You can circle downtown by turning right on First Avenue, then left on Lula Road and back to Main Street. Or you can take a lap on the track around Lilburn City Park.

HIGHLIGHTS

The wide, well-maintained sidewalk on Camp Creek Road is an all-star. Downtown Lilburn has preserved its rich history and is home to several long-standing, family-owned stores. Visit with one of the merchants to hear all about the past, present, and future of Lilburn.

KEEP IN MIND

Behave while in the park; the police station is less than 500 yards away.

NEARBY NOTABLES

Visit the antiques, crafts, and consignment stores in downtown Lilburn. There are basketball courts, playground equipment, and a baseball field at the Lilburn City Park for those looking for an alternative to running. While downtown Lilburn does not offer any food and beverage sources, there's an array of fast-food restaurants and convenience stores on Lawrenceville Highway to meet your energy needs.

STONE MOUNTAIN
Runnin' around the Rock

DISTANCE
5.0 and 8.0 miles,
8.0 and 12.8 kilometers (loop)

HILL FACTOR
Nonexistent

GETTING THERE
Approximately 16 miles east of downtown. Take I-285 to Stone Mountain Freeway/Highway 78 (exit 39B) and go east to the main entrance at exit 8.

PARKING
Parking is available in lots for a fee of $7.00 per vehicle. The park also offers an annual permit for $30.00. Should you wish to run or bike into the park, the nearest free parking is in the Village of Stone Mountain, approximately 1.0 mile away.

OVERVIEW
Stone Mountain, the world's largest mass of exposed granite, rises more than 800 feet. Geologists estimate it has taken more than 300 million years of erosion and weathering in order to reveal the mountain. Today, the granite face displays the sculpted likenesses of three Confederate generals, Robert E. Lee, Stonewall Jackson, and Jefferson Davis. The carving on Stone Mountain began in 1915 under the direction of Gutzon Borglum, the artist better known for his later work on Mount Rushmore. However, due to numerous financial and operational woes, the carving was not completed until 1970, fifty-five years, and five sculptors later. The route also passes other park attractions, including the Grist Mill, Confederate Hall, Riverboat Complex, and Antebellum Plantation.

THE COURSE
MAIN ROUTE: The lightly traveled roads inside the park showcase Georgia's most famous natural wonder and number one tourist attraction and also provide a couple of fabulous loop runs. Both are entirely on wide, well-maintained sidewalks. Simply start your run on the sidewalk and return to your starting point. Robert E. Lee Boulevard nets you 5.0 miles; incorporate Stonewall Jackson Drive and Jefferson Davis Drive to get an addtional 3.0 miles. Both options can be started from anywhere within the

STONE MOUNTAIN PARK

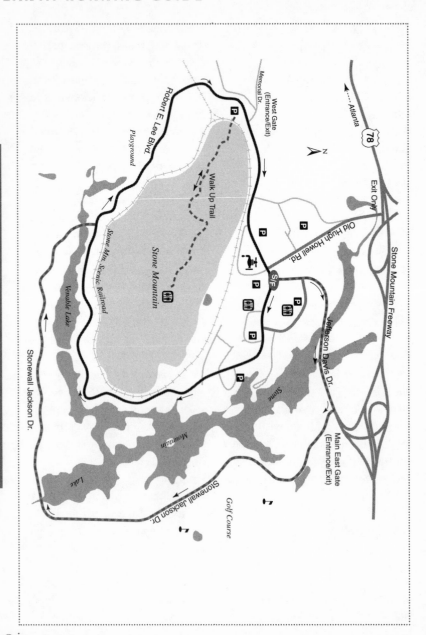

park and provide dramatic views of Stone Mountain from all sides. Despite the elevation of Stone Mountain itself, the terrain around it is predominantly flat, with some gently rolling areas thrown in for good measure. The park entrance fee includes a map that will reinforce how simple it is to follow the suggested routes.

ALTERNATE: You can easily add up to 10 miles of hiking trails or a 1.3-mile walk-up trail to the top of Stone Mountain to your agenda.

HIGHLIGHTS

Plenty of options are available for non-runners in the group, including two fabulous golf courses, a world-class tennis center, a large playground complete with equipment separated by skill levels, and a lake that is perfect for the local fishing enthusiast. In case of an emergency, police call boxes are located throughout the park.

KEEP IN MIND

The park entrance fee is $7.00 *per vehicle*, not per person. You may run or bike into the park to avoid the parking fees. Park gates open at 6:00 AM. Closing times vary according to the season. Avoid arriving at the park's main gate or west gate near laser show times in the summer because traffic is heavy and parking spaces are scarce. For general information, call 770-498-5690, or visit their website at www.stonemountainpark.com.

NEARBY NOTABLES

Plenty of full-service concessions, restaurants, and rest rooms are located on the park grounds. During the summer, complete your run in time to have an evening picnic on the lawn below the carving and take in the laser show that starts at dusk.

31

AVONDALE ESTATES
A Quick and Quiet Quest

DISTANCE
3.0 miles, 4.8 kilometers (loop)

HILL FACTOR
Moderate

GETTING THERE
Approximately 7.5 miles east of downtown. Take I-85 to Clairmont Road and go south. Turn left on Commerce Drive, then left on East College Avenue, which becomes North Avondale Road. Turn right on Clarendon Avenue, then left onto Avondale Plaza South, then to the start at Kensington Drive.

PARKING
Curbside parking is allowed on many, but not all, of the streets in Avondale Estates; some are restricted to residents only. The police are vigilant about ticketing abusers, so pay attention to the signs.

PUBLIC TRANSPORTATION
The area is served by the Mountain Industrial (#121)

MARTA bus, which departs from the Avondale Station.

OVERVIEW
Avondale Estates, a quiet secluded neighborhood, lies just inside I-285. East of Decatur, this community brings a diverse collection of houses together harmoniously. A small, well-maintained lake with ducks and an occasional heron provides a perfect centerpiece for those wishing to log a few moderate miles on foot.

THE COURSE
MAIN ROUTE: Start at the triangle intersection of Kensington Drive, Berkeley Road, and Avondale Plaza South. Head south and downhill on Berkeley Road for about 0.75-mile, alongside Lake Avondale. When you reach Wiltshire Boulevard, cross carefully to the asphalt-paved path marked "Motorized Vehicles Prohibited." This path passes through a bird sanctuary and reconnects with Berkeley Road. The next 1.0 mile is a gradual climb toward Avondale High School, near the intersection with Clarendon Road. Turn right on Clarendon, and cross Wiltshire again. Clarendon ends in patriotic fashion with its surface painted with red, white, and blue

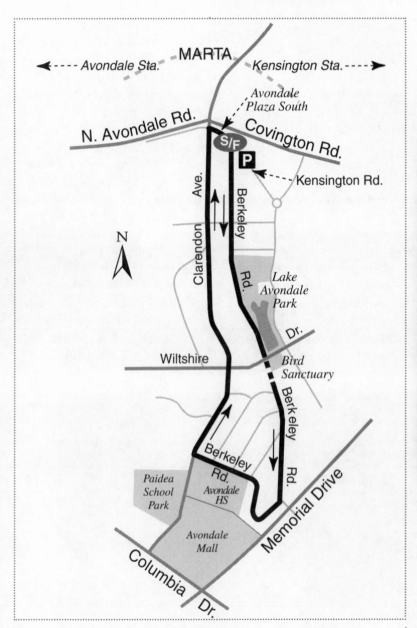

stars. Upon reaching South Avondale Drive, you will be one thousand yards east of the starting point.

HIGHLIGHTS

Lake Avondale is home to a variety of interesting waterfowl. It is generally unnecessary to use any of the neighborhood sidewalks, as traffic is light, and drivers are conscientious and courteous. The starting point of this run is near the former home of Gutzon Borglum, one of the most talented "quitters" in the history of Atlanta (note the Department of the Interior historical marker). The original sculptor hired to do the carving on Stone Mountain (entry 30), Borglum abandoned the project and his home in Avondale Estates after a dispute

with the Stone Mountain Memorial Association in 1925. His reputation was salvaged at his next destination, South Dakota, where he designed and executed the carving of Mount Rushmore.

KEEP IN MIND

The lighting on various sections of the street is poor, making it a route best suited for daylight hours.

NEARBY NOTABLES

Downtown Avondale has a neat, if small, collection of boutiques and galleries. The Avondale Pizza Cafe serves up a good pie in an atmosphere plenty casual for any harrier still in running gear.

DECATUR
Where the Running Is Greater

DISTANCE
5.75 miles, 9.2 kilometers (loop)

HILL FACTOR
Moderate

GETTING THERE
Approximately 6.0 miles east of downtown. Take I-85 to Clairmont Road and go south. Turn right on Commerce Drive, then left on West Trinity Place, then right on North McDonough Street to Agnes Scott College.

PARKING
Curbside parking is available on Ansley Street, one block south of the intersection of McDonough Street and College Avenue. There is also a large, usually empty parking lot at the Decatur Church of the Nazarene at the intersection of Ansley and Adams Streets. Parking on the Agnes Scott campus is restricted to students, faculty, and visitors; regulations are strictly enforced.

PUBLIC TRANSPORTATION
The Agnes Scott College campus is located near the Decatur MARTA Station and is also served by the South DeKalb (#15) bus, which departs from the Decatur Station.

OVERVIEW
Decatur's downtown business and entertainment district has been newly energized. The Ponce de Leon Avenue route (entry 19) passes through this area. The best running in Decatur, however, may be in the southern residential section of town.

Agnes Scott College is located on the other side of the tracks from the bustling core of Decatur. The campus of this women's college, created in 1889, is an ideal starting point for a run in the surrounding historic neighborhood. This lesser-known area is locally referred to as the MAK neighborhood, for the three roads that intersect with College Avenue—McDonough Street, Adams Street, and Kings Highway. Downtown Decatur, situated on an elevated ridgeline to the north of campus, seems a world away.

DECATUR

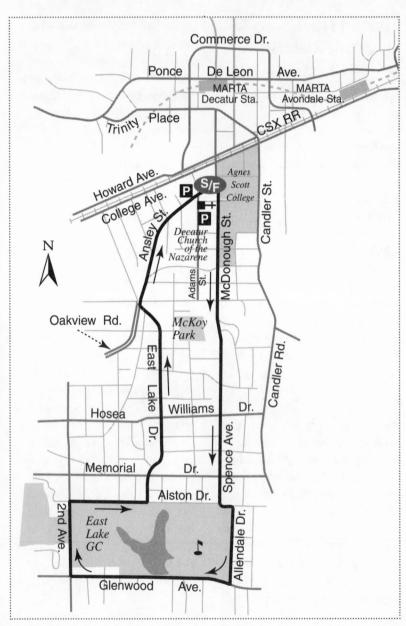

Commerce Dr.

Ponce   De Leon   Ave.

MARTA
Decatur Sta.   MARTA
Avondale Sta.

Trinity   Place

CSX RR

Howard Ave.

College Ave.

Ansley St.

Candler St.

Agnes
Scott
College

S/F

Decatur
Church
of the
Nazarene

McDonough St.

Adams St.

Oakview Rd.

McKoy
Park

East Lake Dr.

Candler Rd.

Hosea   Williams   Dr.

Spence Ave.

Memorial   Dr.

Alston Dr.

2nd Ave.

East
Lake
GC

Allendale Dr.

Glenwood   Ave.

N

THE COURSE

MAIN ROUTE: Start on McDonough Street at College Avenue on the northeast corner of the Agnes Scott College campus and head south on a nice downhill slope for the first 0.5 mile. There is a sidewalk the entire way on McDonough, and vehicular traffic is usually light outside of commuter hours. At the conclusion of the first mile, you enter the city of Atlanta and the road's name changes to Spence Avenue. Sadly, that is not the only change; the sidewalks disappear and the area is somewhat less scenic. Be patient, for this lasts less than 1.0 mile. Continue on Spence Avenue to Memorial Drive. Pay attention: traffic on Memorial is heavy, and there is no traffic signal or crosswalk.

East Lake Golf Club is at the end of Spence Road at Alston Drive, one block south of Memorial Drive. A legendary golf course, East Lake was Bobby Jones's home course. After a history filled with ups and downs, the club returned to prominence when it hosted the 1998 PGA Tour Championship. While the club and grounds are for members only, the surrounding sidewalks offer picturesque views of the course.

Turn left on Alston and then right on Allendale Drive. Follow the contours of the course, turning right on Glenwood Avenue, right on Second Avenue, and a final right to get back on Alston Drive. Look for the main entrance of the golf club on Alston, about 0.5 mile on the right. The beautiful, historic clubhouse is located just south of the intersection of Alston and East Lake Drives.

Turn left on East Lake Drive, passing through the historic East Lake neighborhood. The 5.0-mile point is located in the increasingly trendy Oakhurst section of Decatur. Several streets meet here, including East Lake Drive, Ansley Street, Oakview Road, and Mead Road; there's also an eclectic collection of eateries and pubs. Turn left on Ansley Street and return to McDonough Street.

HIGHLIGHTS

Traffic is very light in the residential areas except during commuter hours. Plenty of trees overhead help diminish the summer's predictable heat. The golf course views are absolutely spectacular.

Renovation and restoration are evident in the mostly historic neighborhoods along the route. A walk on the Agnes Scott campus is a great way to cool down.

KEEP IN MIND

Pay attention to traffic when crossing Memorial Drive and when running Glenwood Avenue—these are major thoroughfares. There is no admittance to East Lake Golf Club without prior arrangements.

NEARBY NOTABLES

The Oakhurst entertainment district is a great place to meet with friends after your run. For solid or liquid carbohydrates, head to MoJo Pizza, the Universal Joint, or Melton's App & Tap. The Bradley Observatory at Agnes Scott offers a program open to the public on the second Friday evening of the month during the school year. And, of course, downtown Decatur is just to the other side of the tracks.

NORTH FAYETTE
The Runner's Place for Open Space

DISTANCE
6.5 miles or 5.0 miles,
10.4 or 8.0 kilometers (loop)

HILL FACTOR
Moderate

GETTING THERE
Approximately 13 miles from downtown. Take I-85 south to Old National Highway/GA 279 (exit 69) and go south to West Fayetteville Road /GA 314. Turn right on West Fayetteville Road, then right on Kenwood Road, then left on New Hope Road.

PARKING
Several churches with large parking lots line this route.

PUBLIC TRANSPORTATION
There is no public transportation in this area.

OVERVIEW
Most urban runners enjoy stretching their legs on an open country road. Finding such a place in Atlanta has become increasingly difficult. One of the remaining options is the northern portion of Fayette County where there are still lovely views and rural charms. At any time, you might see hay bales, horses, and farmhouses, as well as wooden row and white picket fences in front of spacious wrap-around porches. And all this is less than 10 miles from Atlanta Hartsfield International Airport.

THE COURSE
MAIN ROUTE: This route begins at North Fayette United Methodist Church on New Hope Road, just south of the Kenwood Road intersection. Turn left on New Hope, which takes you past many houses, each situated on one acre or more as required by local ordinance. After 2.0 miles, turn left on White Oak Way and run for exactly 1.0 mile. This is the only road on the route that has stop signs, but the speed limits never exceed 35 miles-per-hour. White Oak Way ends at West Fayetteville Road/GA 314. Turn left, and immediately turn left again on Longview Road.

Mile 4.0 is uphill along Longview Road; you pass Neelys and Phillips Lakes, popular hangouts for local

NORTH FAYETTE

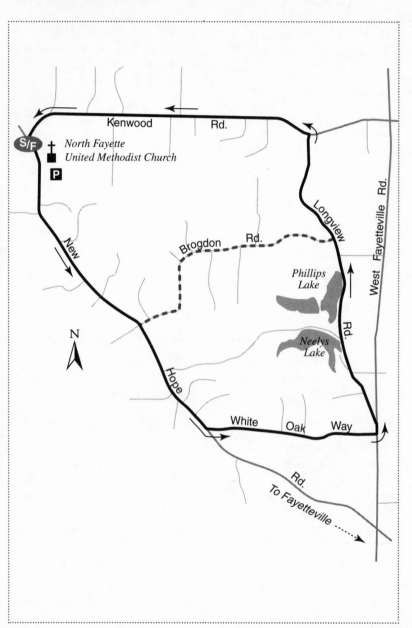

S/F

North Fayette
United Methodist Church

Kenwood Rd.

Longview

West Fayetteville Rd.

New

Brogdon Rd.

Phillips Lake

Neelys Lake

Rd.

N

Hope

White Oak Way

Rd.

To Fayetteville

anglers. The approaching canopy of trees is almost tunnel-like. The road ends just shy of 5.0 miles at Kenwood Road. Turn left on Kenwood, and continue for about 1.5 miles, mostly uphill. Turn left when you reach New Hope Road, and return to your starting point.

ALTERNATE: If you prefer a 5.0-mile trek, turn left on Brogdon Road from New Hope Road instead of continuing to the bend at White Oak Way. Brogdon Road ends at Longview Road. Turn left to rejoin the route and follow the directions given above.

HIGHLIGHTS

This suggested route is just one example of the great country roads to run in Fayette County. Many of the others require time on one or more state highways in the area to connect with the slower, gentler byways. For your cool down, you can consider throwing a line into Neelys Lake. This is one of the running playgrounds of the South Fulton Running Partners, one of the more fitness- and fellowship-minded organizations in the Road Runners Clubs of America (RRCA).

KEEP IN MIND

There are no sidewalks on any of these country roads. A shoulder is always available, but some have precipitous changeovers. Most of the route is open to sun and rain. Beware of drivers who whiz by, taking advantage of the open roads.

NEARBY NOTABLES

Going south on Highway 314 (near White Oak Way and Longview Road) leads you into Fayetteville, the county seat of Fayette. En route to the historic downtown, you pass almost every type of fast food and casual dining restaurant imaginable.

PEACHTREE CITY
Pedestrian Paradise

DISTANCE
3.5 miles, 5.6 kilometers (loop)

HILL FACTOR
Moderate

GETTING THERE
Approximately 30 miles south of downtown. Take I-85 to Highway 74/Senoia Road (exit 61) and go south to Peachtree Parkway, then east past Lake Kedron. Turn right on Floy Farr Parkway/Highway 54, and go to the Municipal Complex.

PARKING
Although street parking is permitted in many of the Peachtree City neighborhoods, the ideal place to park is in the lot at the Municipal Complex. An adjoining parking lot is available for the nearby Drake Fields. Both of these lots are open to the public and, with rare exception, able to accommodate all visitors.

PUBLIC TRANSPORTATION
There is no public transportation in this area.

OVERVIEW
Where one begins a run in Peachtree City is the easy part. Less simple is where to end. A community unlike any other in Georgia, Peachtree City is ahead of its time with its affinity for and dependency upon its 90-plus miles of pathways, navigated by golf carts. Golf cart ownership in Peachtree City is second only to Palm Springs, California. Fortunately for pedestrians, however, this distinctive practice in no way discriminates against other users. In fact, cyclists, walkers, and runners make up the largest contingent.

THE COURSE
MAIN ROUTE: The starting point of this route is located at the parking area for the Municipal Complex. Turn left from the parking lot and follow Highway 54 for a short distance and turn left on Willow Bend Road. After an equally short distance, turn left on Hip Pocket Road. After little more than 0.5 mile, the standard sidewalk becomes a golf-cart path and you will see beautiful houses and Lake Peachtree. Hip Pocket Road ends at Kelly Drive; turn left and run alongside the water.

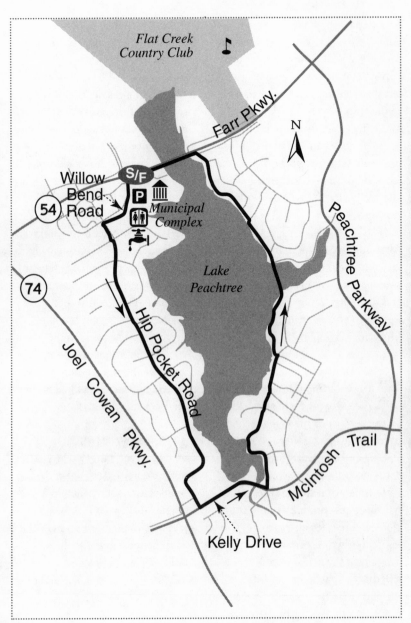

Flat Creek
Country Club

Farr Pkwy.

N

Willow
Bend
Road

54

74

S/F

P

Municipal
Complex

Lake
Peachtree

Peachtree Parkway

Joel Cowan Pkwy.

Hip Pocket Road

McIntosh Trail

Kelly Drive

As you pass the Lake Peachtree dam, Kelly Drive changes names to McIntosh Trail. Shortly after the name changes, you see a path to the left that runs perpendicular to the road. Turn onto this path and head along the east side of the lake past the boat docks and a couple of fishing spots. This path is not along the road, but instead between the water and the backyards of neighborhood residents.

After 3.0 miles, you return to Highway 54. Use the path that takes you over the Lake Peachtree bridge, and then turn left on Highway 54. Return to your starting point at the Municipal Complex.

HIGHLIGHTS
All paths are at least eight feet wide and many of them are shaded by trees. Most of the neighborhood streets have light traffic and wide layouts and are nearly as accommodating to pedestrians as the paths. Path users, regardless of their mode of transportation, are usually courteous and respectful. Peachtree City residents always seem happy to help orient those lost in the labyrinth of passageways. Many of the path-road intersections have pedestrian tunnels or bridges. The

Peachtree City Running Club has installed markers for their most popular 10K course as well as the route around Lake Peachtree. If you wish to join a resident for a run, visit the Peachtree City Running Club at www.ptcrc.com. They have a plethora of fun activities on the calendar and enthusiastically welcome visitors.

KEEP IN MIND
It is easy to get disoriented because the off-road passageways tirelessly crisscross one another; it is helpful to keep specific landmarks in mind. No public rest rooms are available on the paths, but it is acceptable to use those in the public library at the Municipal Complex. Because of their quiet motors, golf carts can appear suddenly; monitor path users accordingly!

NEARBY NOTABLES
The Wyndham Peachtree Conference Center on Highway 54 is 0.5 mile east of the Municipal Complex. It has some pleasing dining and drinking options and offers complimentary maps of the Peachtree City pathways.

View from

atop Pigeon Hill

in the Kennesaw

Mountain

National

Battlefield

Park

THE TRAILBLAZERS

SWEETWATER CREEK

DISTANCE
5.0 and 3.0 miles,
8.0 and 4.8 kilometers (loop)

HILL FACTOR
Extreme

GETTING THERE

Approximately 15 miles west of downtown. Take I-20 west to Thornton Road (exit 44) and go south to Blairs Bridge Road, then west to Mt. Vernon Road, and south into the park. Once inside the park, go east on Factory Shoals Road and follow the signs to Old Manchester Ruins Nature Trails.

PARKING

Plenty of parking is available inside the park and at the trailheads. The park entrance fee is $2.00, except on Wednesdays when parking at all Georgia state parks is free.

PUBLIC TRANSPORTATION

There is no public transportation in this area.

OVERVIEW

Sweetwater Creek State Conservation Park is home to the some of the most enjoyable—but not easiest—trail running in metropolitan Atlanta. You are assured an abundance of solitude and will be surrounded by fascinating vegetation, wildlife, and unique topographical features created by a fault zone that runs directly through the Sweetwater Creek basin. You can see the remains of the New Manchester Mill, which was destroyed by Union forces during the Civil War. The trails are challenging, but manageable, and always well marked. There are plenty of fallen trees to hurdle, footbridges to cross, and more than a couple of hills that will make you earn the spectacular views from the top.

THE COURSE

MAIN ROUTE: The longer of the two routes combines wildlife trails that are clearly marked with blue and then white blazes. This trail begins directly behind the park's ranger station at the blue blazes. You may think, "this ain't too bad" as you descend the first 0.5 mile toward Sweetwater Creek. Be sure to watch your footing, however,

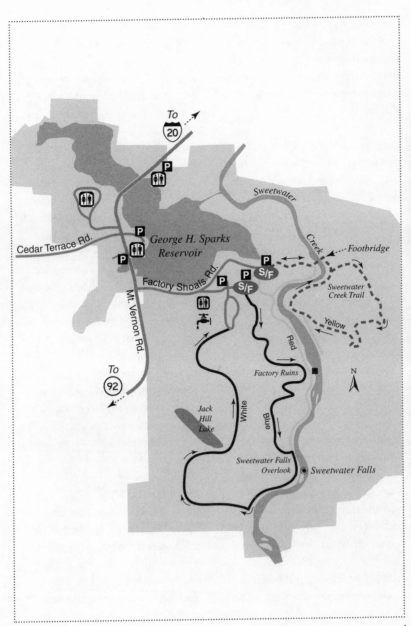

To
20

Sweetwater

P

P

Creek

···Footbridge

Cedar Terrace Rd.

P
George H. Sparks
Reservoir

P

P

P

P

S/F

S/F

Factory Shoals Rd.

Sweetwater
Creek Trail

Yellow

Mt. Vernon Rd.

Red

To
92

Factory Ruins

N

White

Jack
Hill
Lake

Blue

Sweetwater Falls
Overlook

Sweetwater Falls

as there are plenty of exposed treacherous roots. And it seems—especially on the downhills—that if the roots don't get you, the jagged rocks protruding from the ground just might.

Once you reach the creek and the mill ruins, follow the blue blazes back into the interior of the park. Before returning to the creek and the Sweetwater Falls overlook at mile 2.0, you'll encounter a series of climbs, including one card-carrying member of the lung-bustin' club. As you make the transition to white blazes, you find yourself parallel to, and within a few feet of, the creek. You need to execute some fancy footwork and exercise caution and patience. A most tortuous ascent awaits you. The reward at the top is great, however, as you take in Jack's Hill Lake. The white blazes are supplemented by directional arrows on metal posts for the last 2.0 miles as you make your way back to the ranger station and past the staff residences and picnic areas. You use both trails and park service roads for this final leg.

ALTERNATE: The second Sweetwater Creek run is 2.0 miles shorter, but certainly not any easier. In fact, the

inclines and declines on the east side trail, marked with yellow blazes, are actually steeper. Begin this route at the bottom of the parking lot near Group Shelter 7. Once again, you start with an enjoyable descent that lulls you into a false sense of ease. At the bottom, the trail meanders within earshot of the creek to Ferguson's M-6 Bridge. After you cross the bridge, you can go either right or left, but make sure that you choose a yellow-blazed trail and not the park service road. Regardless of your choice, you will ascend a hill with a grade and distance that challenges even the heartiest of trail runners. It is followed by 0.5 mile of relatively level footing before a descent that allows for controlled or breakneck speed—you get to choose—that returns you to the beginning of the loop. Retrace your footsteps across the bridge and back to your start at the parking lot.

HIGHLIGHTS

There are maps at every trailhead. Placards along the wildlife trails identify many of the plant and wildlife species. The scenery and surroundings are amazing. Activities for non-runners include hiking, fishing, and picnicking.

KEEP IN MIND

The park trails close at sunset. It is illegal for guests to pick flowers or collect any other items (except trash) along the trails in any of Georgia's state parks.

NEARBY NOTABLES

The best option for post-run replenishment is to bring a picnic and enjoy it with family or friends in the park. There are some gas station convenience stores and a Fiesta Mexican restaurant on Thornton Road. Farther afield on Lee Road, one exit west of Thornton Road on I-20, are other convenience stores and a Waffle House.

RED TOP MOUNTAIN

DISTANCE
5.5 miles, 8.8 kilometers (loop)

HILL FACTOR
Significant

GETTING THERE
Approximately 35 miles northeast of downtown. Take I-75 north to Red Top Mountain Road (exit 285) and go east into the park.

PARKING
Parking is available in designated areas throughout the park. Although occasionally unavailable, the most convenient parking is at the visitors center. A $2.00 parking fee or annual permit is required for all vehicles (except on Wednesdays, when parking at all Georgia state parks is free).

PUBLIC TRANSPORTATION
There is no public transportation in this area.

OVERVIEW
Red Top Mountain State Park is named for the soil's rich, red color, which is caused by the high iron ore content. Located on lovely Lake Allatoona, the park contains a total of 12 miles of trails, all suitable for running. The Homestead Trail is the best of all: challenging terrain, beautiful surroundings, sure footing, and an easy-to-follow route. It also begins and ends, conveniently, at the park's visitors center.

THE COURSE
MAIN ROUTE: The Homestead Trail trailhead is just to your left as you enter the visitors center. It is marked accordingly and identified by yellow blazes the entire length of the trail. At the onset, you may believe you are in for a stroll in the park as the first 0.5 mile descends gradually over such yielding surfaces as woodchips and pine straw. Be careful; roots and embedded rocks lurk underneath. As you pass the 1.0-mile mark and approach the Lodge Road crossing, the trail rolls, not always gently, and ascends more than descends.

On the north side of Lodge Road, a sign indicating the Homestead Trail loop marks the place for a decision about which way to go. The clockwise route offers the most significant

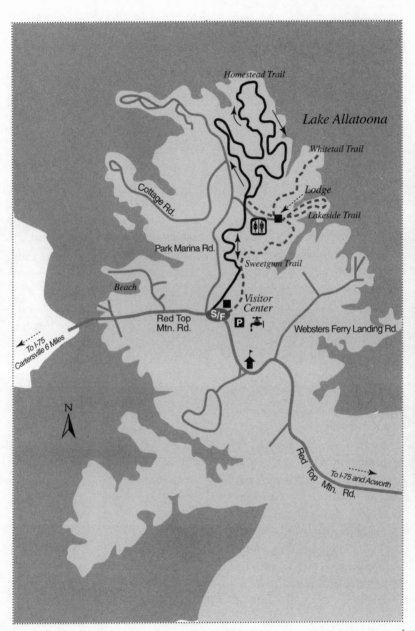

Homestead Trail

Lake Allatoona

Whitetail Trail

Cottage Rd.

Lodge

Lakeside Trail

Park Marina Rd.

Sweetgum Trail

Beach

Visitor Center

S/F

To I-75
Cartersville 6 Miles

Red Top Mtn. Rd.

P

Websters Ferry Landing Rd.

N

Red Top Mtn. Rd.

To I-75 and Acworth

hill work and the best lake views. The opposite direction presents a slightly easier (everything is relative) jaunt and mileage markers. Regardless of your choice, there are beautiful, secluded coves on Lake Allatoona and dense, hardwood forest for the duration of the loop. After completing the 3.5-mile loop, you arrive back at the spur trail from which you departed. Retrace your steps, or for a slightly longer run, switch to the Sweetgum Trail (clearly marked near Lodge Road and identified with red blazes) to make your return. The Sweet Gum Trail adds just over 0.5 mile and also leads you to the visitors center.

ALTERNATE: Other shorter trails, including Lakeside and White Tail, make it easy to incorporate additional distance.

HIGHLIGHTS
Deer are regularly seen along the Homestead and Sweet Gum Trails. There are mileage markers on the Homestead Trail. Portable toilets are located in the parking lot of the visitors center. Free trail maps are available in the visitors center.

KEEP IN MIND
Some lower areas of the trails do not shed water well after heavy rainfalls. Use caution on the two required crossings of Lodge Road.

NEARBY NOTABLES
A swim at Red Top's Lake Allatoona provides a summer cool-off. There are numerous fast food and convenience stores along the exits on I-75. At the Red Top Mountain exit, there is a Texaco gas station with a FoodMart.

KENNESAW MOUNTAIN

DISTANCE
5.0, 10.0, and 16.0 miles,
8.0, 16.0, and 25.6 kilometers
(all loops)

HILL FACTOR
Moderate

GETTING THERE
Approximately 19 miles north-west of downtown. Take I-75 north to Barrett Parkway (exit 269), go southwest to Old Highway 41, and then southeast to Stilesboro Road and turn right. The park's visitors center is on your left.

PARKING
Free parking is available at the visitors center or at any of the trail-heads. On weekends, only park shuttles are allowed on the road to the overlook.

PUBLIC TRANSPORTATION
The area is served by the #45 Cobb Community Transit (CCT) bus.

OVERVIEW
Kennesaw Mountain National Battlefield Park was the site of one of the Civil War's bloodiest battles. More than 3,000 soldiers perished during General Sherman's March to the Sea. Now, this beautiful park is home to well-marked paths and plenty of activity areas. With the recent growth of metropolitan Atlanta, however, longtime residents may not appreciate the recent ex-plosion in its popularity. Every day, and especially on spring and sum-mer weekends, the visitors center and parking lots are filled. Fortu-nately for the runner, after the first 1.5 miles to the Kennesaw Moun-tain overlook, the trails are free of congestion.

THE COURSE
The park trails comprise a series of loops. If you know your way around on the local roads, you can begin your run from any of the trailheads. Despite the potential parking headache, I suggest you start at the visitors center. This will require you to climb Kennesaw Mountain to reach the park's inte-rior. The summit is a healthy 1.5-mile climb with some extremely steep grades. Many runners choose

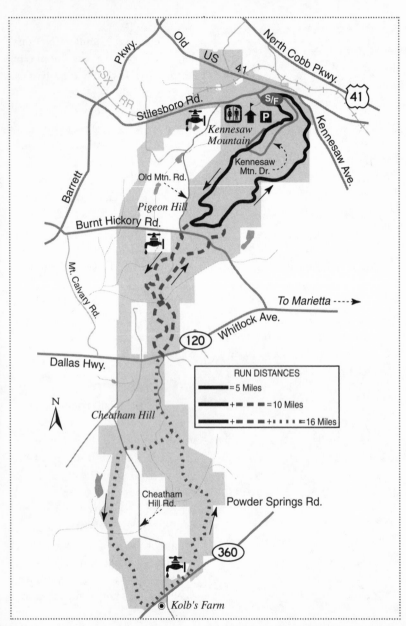

RUN DISTANCES

= 5 Miles

+ = = = = 10 Miles

+ = = = + · · · · = 16 Miles

Kennesaw Mountain

Kennesaw Mtn. Dr.

Old Mtn. Rd.

Pigeon Hill

Burnt Hickory Rd.

Mt. Calvary Rd.

To Marietta - - - - ▶

Whitlock Ave.

120

Dallas Hwy.

N

Cheatham Hill

Cheatham Hill Rd.

Powder Springs Rd.

360

Kolb's Farm

Stilesboro Rd.

Barrett

Pkwy.

Old

US

41

North Cobb Pkwy.

41

Kennesaw Ave.

CSX

RR

S/F

to join the majority of visitors in a walk to the top as a warm-up, before picking up a quicker pace on the other side. Regardless of your decision, this first part is often crowded, but the wide path makes for few traffic jams.

5.0 MILES Once past the overlook, begin your descent past Confederate trenches. The trail to Pigeon Hill is narrower, less populated, and more technical than its predecessor. It also has the standard hazards of off-road running—roots, rocks, and uneven footing. Pay extra attention during the portion of the trail from Little Kennesaw Mountain starting at 2.25 miles. It is steep, rocky, and downright treacherous. If you wish to limit your run to 5.0 miles, take the path at Pigeon Hill (marked by a sign) that begins the loop back to the visitors center. If you get to Burnt Hickory Road, you've missed it.

10.0 MILES From Pigeon Hill to Dallas Highway, the path widens and becomes less threatening. In some instances, Mother Nature has paved your way with a soft bed of pine straw. As you pass more Confederate earthworks, you see even fewer pedestrians. Although the steepest climbs and descents are behind you, this part of the trail rolls continuously, sometimes less than gently. If you only want to go 10.0 miles, reverse your direction by taking the intersecting trail north near the juncture with Dallas Highway (GA 120).

16.0 MILES After you cross Dallas Highway, the trail makes its way toward Cheatham Hill and, eventually, Kolb's Farm, and then it loops back, so you don't have to watch for other trails to make your return. Not surprisingly, it is in this portion, passing through hardwood forests, wetlands, and sprawling meadows, where you find the most solitude. On the far side of Cheatham Hill Road, you occasionally encounter equestrians and their steeds, as riding is permitted in this section of the park. The trail itself never actually passes Kolb's Farm (the farthest point from the visitor center) although you can see it when you cross back over Cheatham Hill Road near the Powder Springs Road intersection.

HIGHLIGHTS

Trail maps are free at the visitors center. There are signs on the trail for Cheatham Hill, Kolb's Farm, and the visitors center. On clear days, you can see the Atlanta skyline from the overlook. The activity areas and visitors center offer options for the non-runners in your group. No need for sunglasses here; the entire trail is shaded by trees.

KEEP IN MIND

Please stay on the trails and off all earthworks and artillery replicas. When approaching a horse and rider ahead of you on the trail, make sure that they are aware of your presence—and pass *slowly*. When an oncoming horse and rider approaches, stop, step to the side of the trail, be still, and allow them to proceed. Resume running only after they are ten or more yards beyond you.

NEARBY NOTABLES

Water fountains are available at trail intersections near Burnt Hickory Road and Powder Springs. Vending machines and rest rooms are located in the visitors center. Dining and drinking establishments can be found on Barrett Parkway on the way to or from the park.

CHATTAHOOCHEE RIVER NATIONAL RECREATION AREA

The Chattahoochee River is a 540-mile waterway that flows from the north Georgia mountains through Atlanta to the Georgia/Florida/Alabama state line.

Since 1978, the Department of the Interior, with the support of local conservation-minded citizen groups, has ensured federal protection for much of the remaining undeveloped land on the river's shoreline in or near Atlanta by regularly acquiring riverfront acreage and incorporating it into the Chattahoochee River National Recreation Area (NRA). Today, the Chattahoochee River NRA includes almost a dozen different units, encompasses more than 300 acres of land, and contains over 70 miles of trails.

The trail running options around this waterway, whose name comes from the Cherokee Indian term meaning "River of the Painted Rocks," are as plentiful as they are diverse. And because each unit in

the Chattahoochee River NRA is completely separate from the others, many north Atlanta residents are relatively close to one or more trails. The following information begins with the southernmost unit and concludes with the northernmost. For additional information about these units, contact the Superintendent, Chattahoochee River National Recreation Area, 1978 Island Ford Parkway, Atlanta, GA 30350-3400. General park information can be obtained by calling 770-399-8070 or 770-952-4419 or by visiting their website at www.nps.gov/chat.

Some units—Medlock Bridge, Abbot's Bridge, Suwanee Creek, and McGinnis Ferry—are not included because trail conditions, ongoing vegetative rehabilitation, or limited trail availability make them less desirable for running.

WEST PALISADES UNIT

DISTANCE
2.5 or 4.0 miles,
4.0 or 6.4 kilometers (loop)

HILL FACTOR
Significant

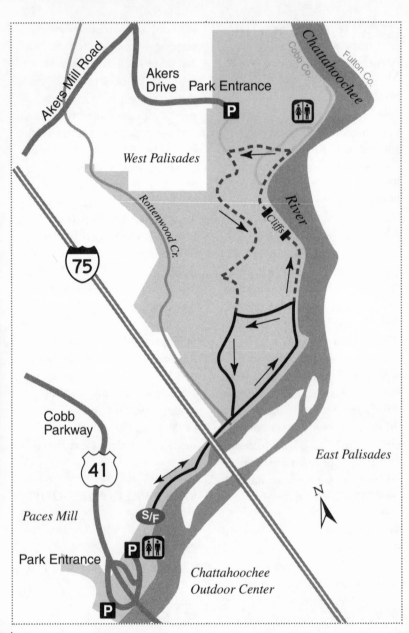

Akers Mill Road

Akers Drive

Park Entrance

West Palisades

Rottenwood Cr.

Chattahoochee

Cobb Co.

Fulton Co.

River

Cliffs

75

Cobb Parkway

41

Paces Mill

East Palisades

S/F

Park Entrance

Chattahoochee Outdoor Center

N

GETTING THERE

Approximately 10 miles northwest of downtown. Take I-75 to Mount Paran Road (exit 256); go south to Northside Parkway/US 41. Take US 41-North to the entrance.

PARKING

There is a large parking area for the recreation field and trailhead. All Chattahoochee Recreation units require a $2.00 parking fee or a $25.00 annual parking permit.

PUBLIC TRANSPORTATION

The area is served by the #10 Cobb County Transit (CCT) bus, which departs from the MARTA Arts Center Station.

OVERVIEW

This unit serves as the take-out point for river rafters "shootin' the 'Hooch;" the river becomes more dangerous and unpredictable downstream. The same can be said for the trails that follow the river. Although more suitable for running, there is a portion of the route that is given to nontechnical rock climbing and scrambling.

THE COURSE

MAIN ROUTE: The trail begins behind the recreation field on a soft, wide cover of pea gravel. Travel on this surface for about 0.5 mile, going underneath I-75 and along the river. At the footbridge over Rottenwood Creek, the party's over. While you can choose to go either right or left, it's easier and safer to climb up the impending cliffs on the right than it is to come down them. From here, the trail continuously narrows, tossing in an ever-increasing number of sharp rocks and exposed roots. The view of the river, especially in the winter when the dense greenery is absent, is a reward for your efforts.

At about 1.0 mile, the trail forks. To run 2.5 miles and avoid the cliffs, go left. This route will take you almost 0.5 mile to an old forest service road. Another left turn gets you back to the previously mentioned footbridge and the return trip to the parking lot.

ALTERNATE: If you are interested in the 4.0-mile route and a respite from the running, take the right fork. The cliffs are 0.25 mile ahead of the fork. You cannot miss them nor can you avoid them (unless you plan on getting wet). In certain places, you may need to use your hands to help pull yourself up

141

the rocks. At the end of the rock climbing, you come to a couple of trail options. To avoid losing the main route, always take the option that continues the ascent. Eventually, you come to a forest road and a posted trail map. Turn left and proceed with caution, as the road back to Rottenwood Creek is a 1.0-mile treacherous downhill grade, complete with uneven footing every step of the way. The last 0.5 mile is the same gentle path that brought you from the recreation field and the starting point.

HIGHLIGHTS
Provided they don't intimidate you, the cliffs are a wonderful diversion. Despite its ideal location, recreational use of this unit is relatively light. You can hear the sound of the river on the entire eastern side of the route. Trail maps are posted frequently.

KEEP IN MIND
The footing along this route is not for beginners. The National Park Service, as well as fellow park users, ask that you remain on the designated trails at all Chattahoochee Recreation units. Although getting lost is little more than a potential inconvenience, it is easy to wander off onto certain spur trails along the way.

NEARBY NOTABLES
Riverview Village and the Vinings Junction shopping centers are located on Paces Mill. At Riverview, you can find sandwiches at Blimpie's or burritos, wraps, and salads at Cactus Moon. Vinings Junction is the site of The Pizza Construction Company with its "pocket" pizza. Lassiter's Tavern has both bottled and tap beers. Early morning joggers may enjoy a stop at the Bagel Bin on Cobb Parkway.

EAST PALISADES UNIT

DISTANCE
3.0 or 5.0 miles,
4.8 or 8.0 kilometers (loop)

HILL FACTOR
Significant

GETTING THERE
Approximately 10 miles northwest of downtown. Take I-75 to Mount Paran Road (exit 256), and go northeast to Harris Trail, then north to Northside Drive, then north to Indian Trail. Turn left on Indian Trail and follow it into the park.

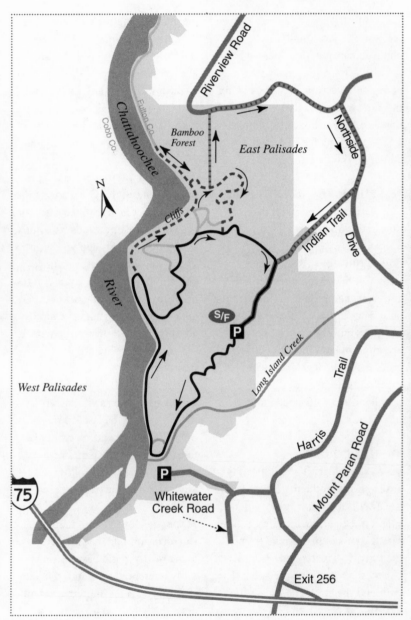

EAST PALISADES UNIT

PARKING

A relatively small, rarely busy, unpaved parking lot is located at the trailhead. Additional parking is permitted in certain locations along the park service road. All Chatta- hoochee Recreation units require a $2.00 parking fee or a $25.00 annual parking permit.

PUBLIC TRANSPORTATION

There is no public transporta- tion in this area.

OVERVIEW

You'll find some rewarding and challenging trail running at this unit. The cliffs provide the greatest obstacles and the greatest sense of accomplishment, but slow your ground speed considerably. In fact, the middle distance of this route is a walk on the wild side, and not for everyone.

THE COURSE

MAIN ROUTE: The trailhead is at the corner of the main East Pal- isades parking lot. It begins on a single-track path, which descends rapidly. Less than 1.0 mile from the start, you reach Long Island Creek, the route's lowest point. The path and the creek soon meet the Chattahoochee River, and the trail

meanders along the river for 1.0 mile, sometimes at the edge of the water. The path is very narrow in places and presents the expected hazards of protruding rocks, roots, and uneven footing. Not surpris- ingly, your proximity to the water results in terrific views.

After about 1.0 mile from the point where Long Island Creek meets the Chattahoochee, a trail retreats from the floodplain and heads back into the woodlands. Should you wish to avoid the cliffs, take this trail. As you climb, you will encounter a few other trails splintering off in differ- ent directions. Fortunately, almost all of them lead toward the same place, and there are ample trail maps along the way that show your current position. As you might expect from your swift descent at the beginning, the last 1.0 mile is all uphill. The trail widens gradually until you reach the park entrance road. Turn right and follow the gravel road to the parking area.

ALTERNATE: If you want a 5.0-mile run incorporating the cliffs, continue along the river and past the previ- ously referenced trails into the inte- rior. As you enter the cliff and bluff area, the light blue blazes on the trees give way to green blazes on trees, rocks, roots—whatever is available—as you move upward. In this section, you won't be running; you will be walking, climbing, and crawling. You'll have leaves in your hair, bugs in your clothes, and dirt underneath your fingernails. You will encounter ledges with long drops. You may regularly question your footing and you might lose the trail's green markings. Hopefully, you will enjoy every minute of it. Regardless, you'll come to a wooden overlook. Savor the spectacular view up the mouth of the river and know that now you will be able to do some trail running again.

The trail finally returns to the water's edge near the ruins of a cabin from the early 1900s. Be on the lookout for the next trail away from the river, for it is the road home. (If you wish, stay on the path along the river a short while longer, crossing over a footbridge and entering one of the few remaining bamboo forests in the area. Past this point, the trail is confusing and poorly maintained and, ultimately, a dead end.) The correct trail leads back to an old forest service road. To stay on the trails and eliminate some of the time on the forest road,

be on the lookout for a trail about 0.5 mile up on the right side of the forest road. Follow this path, always going to the right when presented with a choice, for a little over 0.5 mile to reach the gravel road park entranceway. Another right turn takes you the short distance to the lot. If you miss the necessary right on the forest service road, you will reach Riverview Road. In this case, incorporate a little road running into the journey by going right on Riverview Road to Northside Drive. Turn right at Northside Drive and follow it a short distance to Indian Trail. A final right turn on Indian Trail returns you to the parking lot.

HIGHLIGHTS
The views from the shore and the bluffs are fabulous. Even on weekends, the trails deliver a good dose of solitude.

KEEP IN MIND
This trail is not for those who are scared of heights or unaccustomed to crude trail conditions—seriously!

NEARBY NOTABLES
The area surrounding this park is entirely residential. Before or after your run, enjoy a driving

tour of the grand residences and beautiful scenery.

COCHRAN SHOALS/ SOPE CREEK/ POWERS ISLAND UNITS

DISTANCE
3.1 miles, 5.0 kilometers (loop)

HILL FACTOR
Nonexistent (on main loop)

GETTING THERE
Approximately 13 miles northwest of downtown. Take I-285 to Powers Ferry Road/Northside Drive/New Northside Drive (exit 22) and go north on New Northside Drive to Interstate North Parkway. If you are coming from the east, the exit will deposit you on Interstate North Parkway. Cross Powers Ferry Road and follow the signs to the National Recreation Area. If you are coming from the west, follow the signs to New Northside Drive, which crosses over the interstate and leads you to Interstate Parkway and the park entrance.

PARKING
Because the main parking lots for the Cochran Shoals unit also serve as the trailheads, they fill up quickly on weekends and summer evenings. Plenty of overflow parking is available in the Powers Island lot. All Chattahoochee Recreation units require a $2.00 parking fee or a $25.00 annual parking permit.

PUBLIC TRANSPORTATION
The area is served by the Powers Ferry (#148) MARTA bus, which departs from the Sandy Springs Station.

OVERVIEW
The Chattahoochee National Recreation Areas invite measurements that add up to double- or triple-digit numbers: number of units, total miles of trail, and amount of acreage preserved, just to name a few. Surprisingly, however, one consideration that does not make the double digits is the number of trail miles available to a runner at any one unit in the system without having to retrace steps or do multiloops. None of the units has more than 7.5 self-contained miles of trails. And the way the areas are laid out, there is only one series of units that can be connected to increase the total trail mileage available. This lone exception is phenomenal, however; the Cochran Shoals, Sope Creek, and

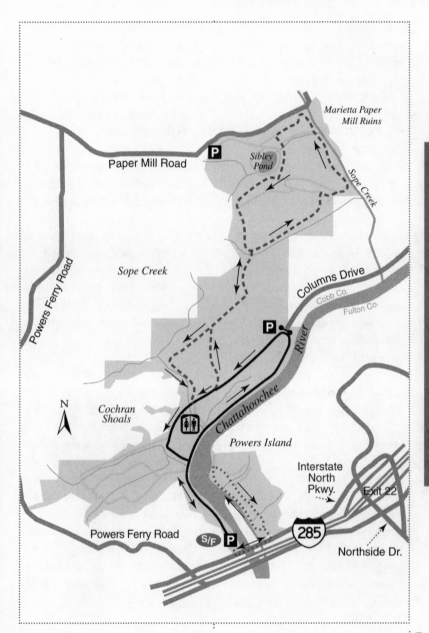

Marietta Paper Mill Ruins

Paper Mill Road

Sibley Pond

Sope Creek

Powers Ferry Road

Sope Creek

Columns Drive

Cobb Co.

Fulton Co.

River

Cochran Shoals

Chattahoochee

Powers Island

N

Interstate North Pkwy.

Exit 22

Northside Dr.

Powers Ferry Road

S/F

285

Powers Island units offer many un-interrupted miles, as well as terrific variations in trail conditions, terrain, and popularity. And all three units can be enjoyed independently.

THE COURSE

COCHRAN SHOALS For good reason, this is the most popular location in the Chattahoochee River NRA. The wide, hard-packed trail provides splendid views of the river, woodlands, marshes, and floodplains. This loop, designed as a fitness trail, is easy to follow and contains more than twenty exercise stations along the way. A trail map is available in both the north and south parking lots. With rare exception, the path is flat and you can run as fast as you wish, depending on the number of other users. The wide-open green spaces and views of the surrounding bluffs provide the perfect finishing touches to your run.

SOPE CREEK You can find a terrific network of side trails within the neighboring Sope Creek unit by exiting one of the two spur trails on the northwest side of the Cochran Shoals loop. Because of elevation changes, these additional trails are considerably more rugged and thus less crowded. Coming from Cochran Shoals into Sope Creek, use the trail option farthest from the Cochran Shoals footbridge. Begin with a 0.7-mile climb that is certainly not for the timid. Within the Sope Creek grounds, there are more than 5.0 miles of trails, including a 3.0-mile loop. This trail keeps you going up and down in the heavily forested area on a relatively wide path, dominated by Georgia red clay, exposed pyrite, and slick rock. Although parts of the trail have plenty of ruts and rocks, the footing is reasonably secure throughout—the only exception being along Sope Creek itself where the trail can be narrow and difficult to navigate.

POWERS ISLAND To reach the Powers Island unit, exit the Cochran Shoals fitness trail on the south side. At the parking lot stop sign, turn left on Interstate Parkway North, and cross the bridge over the Chattahoochee. The first left turn drops you into the Powers Island unit's parking lot. The trailhead is in the back corner of the lot. The available course is a meandering loop route almost 1.5 miles long. The trail also concludes at the Powers Island parking lot about 200 yards from where you began.

HIGHLIGHTS

There is a relatively clean rest room roughly 0.5 mile from the south side parking lot of the Cochran Shoals unit. The Columns Drive route (entry 25) also links directly into this route. All units are equipped with trail maps that indicate your specific position within the park.

KEEP IN MIND

Although the Cochran Shoals trail is wide, it is quite busy at peak times with other runners and walkers (many with dogs or strollers). At the busiest times, parking in the main Cochran Shoals lot can be challenging. Use the Powers Island lot whether or not you plan to run its trails. The Sope Creek unit is popular with local mountain bikers; share the trails accordingly.

NEARBY NOTABLES

You can watch the action on television or from outdoor tables at the Sidelines Sports Bar & Grill on Powers Ferry Road. The pedestrian/cyclist lane along Powers Ferry eliminates the necessity of retrieving your car until after you've refueled.

JOHNSON FERRY NORTH UNIT

DISTANCE
2.5 miles, 4.0 kilometers (loop)

HILL FACTOR
Mild

GETTING THERE

Approximately 14.5 miles from downtown. Take I-285 to Riverside Drive (exit 24), and go north, then west on Johnson Ferry Road to the park.

PARKING

Plenty of parking is available in the designated lot. All Chattahoochee Recreation units require a $2.00 parking fee or a $25.00 annual parking permit.

PUBLIC TRANSPORTATION

There is no public transportation in this area.

OVERVIEW

The Johnson Ferry North unit may be the most underused unit by runners in the entire Chattahoochee River NRA system despite the high quality of trail running conditions. The surrounding foliage is mar-

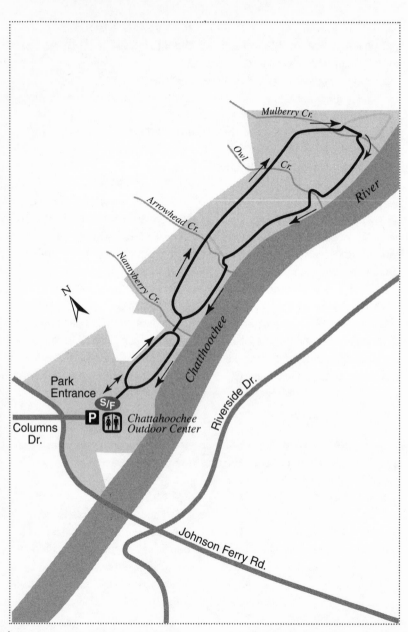

Mulberry Cr.

Owl

Cr.

Arrowhead Cr.

River

Nannyberry Cr.

N

Chattahoochee

Riverside Dr.

Park
Entrance

S/F

P

Chattahoochee
Outdoor Center

Columns
Dr.

Johnson Ferry Rd.

velous and thick, thick, thick, but the paths are clear.

THE COURSE

MAIN ROUTE: This is the northern component of the Johnson Ferry units; Johnson Ferry South offers only short river walks. Johnson Ferry North provides a wonderful 2.5-mile loop that winds through a floodplain forest and passes over several creeks on an easy-to-follow path. Trail maps with position indicators are located throughout, though they are hardly necessary.

HIGHLIGHTS

This trail is always congestion-free. The views and sounds of the river are wonderful. You can connect with the East Cobb/Columns Drive run (entry 25) by crossing Johnson Ferry Road. (Be careful on this busy street.) For even longer jaunts, connect with the trails of Cochran Shoals, Sope Creek and Powers Island units. Rest rooms are available in the parking lot.

KEEP IN MIND

This is a drop-off place for river rafters "shootin' the Hooch," so don't be alarmed by the large number of cars in the parking lot. It's not an indication of trail traffic.

NEARBY NOTABLES

The Chevron gas station, located on Johnson Ferry Road, features a Village Convenience Center stocking runner's pre- and post-run requirements. You probably won't feel comfortable in the other nearby restaurants in your running attire.

GOLD BRANCH UNIT

DISTANCE
4.5 miles, 7.2 kilometers (loop)

HILL FACTOR
Moderate

GETTING THERE

Approximately 15 miles from downtown. Take I-75 north to Marietta Parkway South/GA 120 (exit 263), and go east to Lower Roswell Road, then turn right and go to the park.

PARKING

There is a dirt parking lot at the trailhead. All Chattahoochee Recreation units require a $2.00 parking fee or a $25.00 annual parking permit.

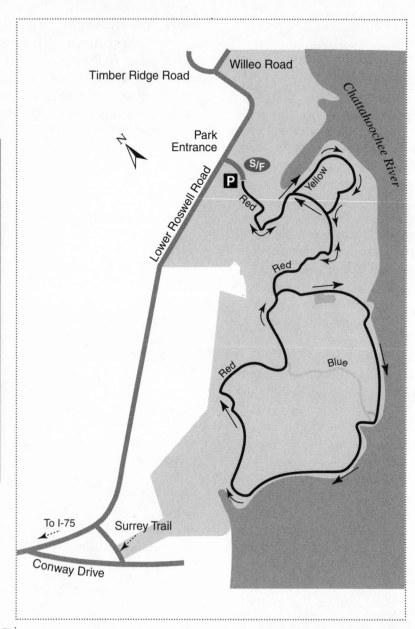

Willeo Road

Timber Ridge Road

Chattahoochee River

Park Entrance

N

S/F

P

Red

Yellow

Lower Roswell Road

Red

Red

Blue

Red

To I-75

Surrey Trail

Conway Drive

PUBLIC TRANSPORTATION

There is no public transportation in this area.

OVERVIEW

Unlike the other units in the Chattahoochee River NRA, the primary attraction at Gold Branch is not the rushing water of the river. Instead, the main draw is the calm and quiet surrounding Bull Sluice Lake, formed after the construction of the Morgan Falls Dam in 1904. This route shows off the lake for almost half of the total distance while offering a challenging course. Fancy footwork, concentration, and good balance are required.

THE COURSE

MAIN ROUTE: From the trailhead, start with a steep, but wide and hazard-free, 0.25-mile descent. As the path levels off, you cross a marshy area on a footbridge. The road forks and is filled with a wealth of trail hazards, including exposed roots, narrow passages, declivitous climbs, and a couple of uneven embankments. Go left after crossing the bridge, which will allow you to avoid a 0.5-mile climb at the beginning of your run. Make your way toward the lake and over another bridge. About 1.0 mile

from the parking lot, you get your first glimpse of the muddy waters of Bull Sluice Lake. The following 2.0 miles take you along the contours of the lake, both high above and down to the edge of the water. At times the trail is wide enough to run side-by-side with a friend. More often, the overgrowth grabs at you and spiderwebs kiss your face. You encounter a few flat parts, more hills, and some steep slopes.

Near 3.0 miles, you will head away from the lake and back into the interior of the park. The next 1.0 mile offers rolling terrain and a wide trail. A relatively significant and extended descent concludes at the footbridge. At the fork, turn left and climb up your original path to return to the parking lot, completing the loop.

HIGHLIGHTS

Thanks to the consistent canopy of trees, shade is guaranteed even on hot, summer days. Despite the central location in a heavily residential area, the park and its trails are rarely busy. Trail maps indicating your position are located at various places along the trail. Shorter distances are possible by taking a couple of alternative routes available through the park's interior.

KEEP IN MIND
There are trail spurs that lead into the interior of the park. Always go to the left in order to complete the suggested route. For safety's sake, keep your eyes on the path, not the water.

NEARBY NOTABLES
Parkaire Landing shopping center is located south on Roswell Road. You'll find several casual, inexpensive restaurants featuring Mexican or Chinese cuisine or New York-style pizza. Convenience stores in the area can provide sports drinks and snacks.

VICKERY CREEK UNIT

DISTANCE
4.25 miles, 6.8 kilometers (loop)

HILL FACTOR
Significant

GETTING THERE
Approximately 19 miles from downtown. Take I-285 to GA 400 (exit 27) to Northridge Road (exit 6) and go west to Roswell Road,

then north to Riverside Road, then east to the park entrance.

PARKING
Parking is available at the trailhead. All Chattahoochee Recreation units require a $2.00 parking fee or a $25.00 annual parking permit.

PUBLIC TRANSPORTATION
The area is served by the Roswell/Alpharetta (#85) MARTA bus, which departs from the North Springs Station.

OVERVIEW
The Vickery Creek Unit provides both a wonderful trail run as well as a glimpse of the area's past, including the decaying ruins of the Roswell mill and dam on acreage that was once home to the Cherokee Nation before the Trail of Tears. While the route is certainly not easy, it is definitely rewarding, both visually and physically.

THE COURSE
MAIN ROUTE: Upon entering the park from the parking lot, look for the modified stairway to your right, a small indication of the climbing to come. The course gains elevation, over rocky and rutted terrain, and leads to an old, wooden foot-

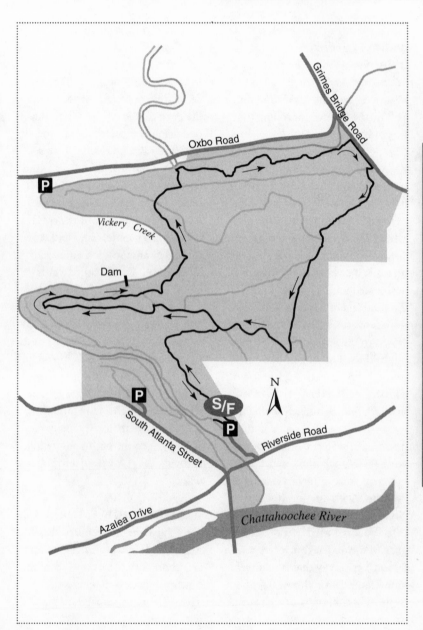

VICKERY CREEK UNIT

bridge. The trail then levels out briefly as you make your way one thousand yards to a T-intersection in the trail. Make a left turn and head west into the park's interior. Follow the 0.5 mile of rolling topography.

Bypass the first spur trail to the right and note (but don't heed) the first orange National Park Service "Notice" recommending that you retrace your route to avoid hazardous conditions. You are not yet on trails that have been closed or designated unsafe. After another 0.5 mile and at another T-intersection, however, go right (the trail is closed to the left), and head downhill to the sound of rushing water. You'll soon come to what is left of the dam built by the Roswell Mill in 1839. Shortly after reaching the lowest point on the trail and after passing the waterfall, look for the steep trail to the right, which will take you back to higher ground and into the park's interior. It will be a climb, more than a run, of about three hundred yards. At the appearance of a wooden row fence, take a left on a pathway that is relatively flat. Continue for almost 0.5 mile to the first trail on your right. Take this trail and ready yourself for

some tricky travel high above Vickery Creek.

In less than 0.5 mile, you'll pass underneath a pedestrian bridge; take the path that heads back into the park's interior for almost 1.0 mile to Grimes Bridge Road. Make a right turn onto Grimes Bridge and continue for a few hundred yards, where you'll see another path that heads back into park territory. Turn into the park and, from here, stay to the left anytime you approach an intersection. One hundred yards from the road you'll find a marker for the "Historic Roswell Trail System," a National Park Service kiosk, and a Vickery Creek map. Keeping to the left will lead you another 1.0 mile back to the almost forgotten wooden footbridge. The remaining trip from the bridge is nothing more than retracing your steps back to the parking lot while enjoying the rewards of a rapid descent.

HIGHLIGHTS
The dam and ruins of the Roswell Manufacturing Company are impressive. The views from the bluffs are no less magnificent. There are plenty of trail maps within the park.

KEEP IN MIND

An additional trail, parallel to this course, is available on the north side of the route. It is narrow, overgrown, subject to flooding, and best avoided. Be careful near the dam. As inviting as the bridge to Waller Park may seem, it provides more than 0.5 mile of added distance.

NEARBY NOTABLES

Taco Mac, a favorite of locals who enjoy hot wings and cold beers, is located less than a mile south on Roswell Road. The North River Shopping Center, further south on Roswell Road, offers the Chicago Pizza Sports Arena and Marquito's Bar & Grill. Quick snacks are available at the Tropical Food Market.

ISLAND FORD UNIT

DISTANCE
3.25 miles, 5.2 kilometers (loop)

HILL FACTOR
Moderate

GETTING THERE

Approximately 17 miles from downtown. From I-285, take GA 400 (exit 27) to Northridge Road (exit 6) and go west to Dunwoody Place, then north to Roberts Drive, then east to Island Ford Parkway.

PARKING

There is plenty of parking at the park headquarters complex, which is also the location of this route's trailhead. All Chattahoochee Recreation units require a $2.00 parking fee or a $25.00 annual parking permit.

PUBLIC TRANSPORTATION

The area is served by the Roswell/Alpharetta (#85) MARTA bus, which departs from the North Springs Station.

OVERVIEW

This park is the Dr. Jekyll and Mr. Hyde of the Chattahoochee River NRA; it offers some of the easiest, most carefree running around, as well as some of the most daunting and challenging trails anywhere in the Atlanta area. With the way this loop is laid out, it's all or nothing.

THE COURSE

MAIN ROUTE: The starting point for this trail is behind the park headquarters complex at the southernmost point of the park. Take the

157

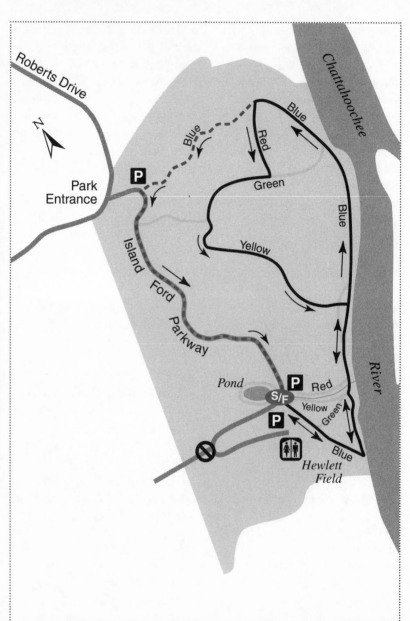

ISLAND FORD UNIT

steep sidewalk down to the Sam Hewlett Recreation Field and head north, away from the boat ramp and along the river, on a flat, wide path covered with a soft, natural bed of pine straw. Stay on the main trail, crossing two footbridges, for a little over 1.0 mile. As you come to the third bridge, your time on Easy Street is drawing to a close and you must make a decision. Regardless of your choice, you'll tap into some of your unused energy.

For a run that is completely off-road, avoid the third bridge and go left at the fork. The path makes a rocky, rutted climb for about 0.5 mile. Reach the summit and follow the yellow blazes and a gently rolling path for another 0.5 mile, followed by a potentially dangerous descent on an uneven, occasionally narrow path, which takes you back to the first footbridge and the riverside. Turn right at this intersection and return to Hewlett Field and the sidewalk that leads to the park headquarters.

For a run that blends trail and road, cross the bridge and make your way toward Island Ford Parkway, the road that brought you into the park. Turn left and run for approximately 2.0 miles; the traffic is light and the drivers are alert. Island Ford Parkway winds through scenic woodlands, showcasing much of the area's native greenery and a picturesque pond. Like the off-road option, it terminates at the park headquarters, but at the front of the building instead of the rear.

ALTERNATE: You can create a wonderful, lengthier run by making multiple loops, incorporating both the off-road and "combo" options. This nets you a total of more than 6.0 miles that is more demanding than almost any local 10K.

HIGHLIGHTS

In addition to the river, great views of Copeland Island are available during the first mile. The park headquarters house the Chattahoochee River National Recreation Area Administrative Offices, the best information source for all Chattahoochee River NRA units. Hours are 8:00 AM–4:30 PM, Monday–Friday. For more information, call 770-952-4419.

KEEP IN MIND

The path along the river can be busy during peak times. Many of the other users are walkers, often accompanied by their canine companions.

NEARBY NOTABLES

The QuikTrip on Dunwoody Place offers an extensive selection of snacks and beverages. On nearby Roswell Road, you'll find a wide variety of dining fare. The Three Dollar Café is a popular and casual spot in the area.

JONES BRIDGE UNIT

DISTANCE
3.0 miles or 6.0 miles, 4.9 or 10.0 kilometers (out and back)

HILL FACTOR
Mild

GETTING THERE

Approximately 22 miles from downtown. Take I-285 to GA 400 (exit 27), to Abernathy Road (exit 5) and go east to Mount Vernon Highway, then northeast. Mount Vernon Highway becomes Mountain Vernon Road and, finally, Spalding Drive. At the intersection of Spalding Drive and Holcomb Bridge Road, go north to Barnwell Road, then east to the park entrance.

PARKING

There is plenty of parking at the park entrance. The first parking lot at the boat ramp is primarily for those with boat trailers. All Chattahoochee Recreation units require a $2.00 parking fee or a $25.00 annual parking permit.

PUBLIC TRANSPORTATION

There is no public transportation in this area.

OVERVIEW

The history of the Jones Bridge makes for an interesting tale. The bridge formerly connected the Fulton and Gwinnett County sides of the Chattahoochee, and was used regularly by area residents for almost thirty years. In the 1930s, however, the bridge was declared unsafe and neither county felt enough civic duty to restore the bridge to working order. The bridge continued to deteriorate until 1940, when half was stolen and supposedly sold as scrap metal!

The trail conditions at Jones Bridge offer the novice trail runner an ideal place to adjust to the off-road

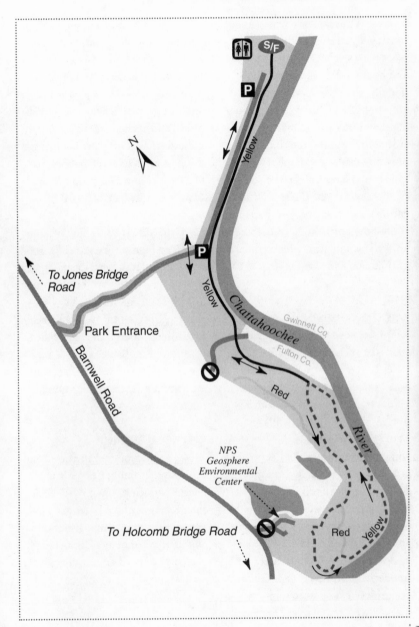

JONES BRIDGE UNIT

lifestyle. The trails are wide enough for two runners, side-by-side, in most places. The surfaces are soft, and home to few hazards. Additionally, the entire trail system is within 0.25 mile of the river, allowing the more casual harrier a regular breather on the riverbanks. The only downside may be that several spur trails, especially in the southern part of the park, test your navigational skills, if not your patience. Although getting hopelessly lost is unlikely, wondering where you are, or how you ended up where you did, is quite possible.

THE COURSE

MAIN ROUTE: The best place to start is at the steel truss ruins of the Jones Bridge in the northernmost area of the park. Follow the river on the trail's main artery, which is well marked with yellow blazes. Many spur trails along the way take you quickly to the water's edge. A little less than 1.0 mile from the start, you come upon the park's boat ramp. The trail resumes on the other side of the ramp's parking lot, and then crosses a creek on a footbridge. Another 0.5 mile later, the trail leads to a gravel road. On the opposite side, you encounter trails marked with red blazes. There are 3.0 miles of trails, including a loop, that pass a scenic pond, and the back entrance to the Geosphere Environmental Education Training Center. If you wish to play it safe and just get in 3.0 miles, begin your return trip at the first red blaze. Otherwise, a good, hard look at the posted trail map is the only prerequisite for continuing on and doubling your distance.

HIGHLIGHTS

The high squirrel and chipmunk population ensures plenty of sounds (and surprises) on the trails as they scavenge for snacks. The entire trail system is well covered by dense greenery. The picnic area near the Jones Bridge ruins is ideal for your post-run rest or for those who are not interested in running the trails.

KEEP IN MIND

The Geosphere Environmental Education Training Center is not generally open to the public. With the exception of the potentially confusing trails, this course is not difficult and thus may not offer enough challenge to hard-core trail runners.

NEARBY NOTABLES

There is an assortment of dining and drinking establishments on Barnwell Road. In the Ellard Village shopping area, you'll find Starbuck's Coffee, Mona Lisa Pizzeria Ristorante, Taco Mac, and Bruster's Ice Cream.

BOWMANS ISLAND UNIT

DISTANCE
3.2 miles, 5.1 kilometers (loop)

HILL FACTOR
Moderate

GETTING THERE

Approximately 28 miles from downtown. From I-285, take GA 400 (exit 27) to Windward Parkway (exit 11) and go west to Cumming Highway, then east to Suwanee Dam Road, then north to Buford Dam Road.

PARKING

Plenty of free parking is available at the Upper Overlook trailhead. Unlike the other Chattahoochee River NRAs, a parking fee or permit is not required.

PUBLIC TRANSPORTATION

There is no public transportation in this area.

OVERVIEW

The Bowmans Island unit is a unique part of the Chattahoochee River NRA. The National Park Service shares the responsibility for maintenance with the U.S. Army Corps of Engineers. As a result, the parking is free. The major attraction in the area is not the Chattahoochee River, but Lake Sidney Lanier. A popular getaway option for many Atlantans, the lake hosts boaters, beach bums, picnickers, water park enthusiasts, and many others every day during the summer and every weekend the rest of the year. Unfortunately for trail runners in Atlanta, while recreational opportunities certainly abound at Lake Lanier, off-road running options are extremely limited. Only one recognized trail, known as the Laurel Ridge Trail, is available on any of the land maintained by the Park Service or Army Corps. While it is definitely worth visiting when you're in the Lake Lanier area, it is probably not worth the trip alone.

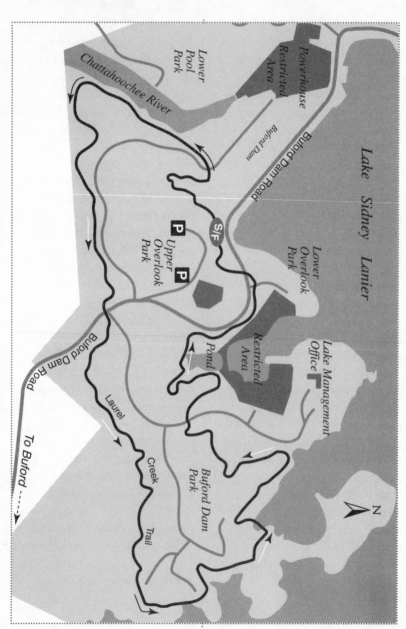

THE COURSE

MAIN ROUTE: The best place to start is at the Upper Overlook, which also happens to be the area that offers the most parking. Begin your jaunt with a gradual-to-steep descent, occasionally getting some impressive views of the Buford Dam, which was completed in 1957 at the cost of $45 million. As the trail flattens out near the 0.5-mile mark, you briefly run alongside the Chattahoochee River. At about 1.0 mile, head east into the woodlands. Mile 2.0 is entirely in the woods; the trail regularly rolls, then crosses over Rocky Creek, taking you through a lush wetland. The final third offers more ascent than descent, crossing numerous roadways and parking lots. Although the entire trail can be somewhat confusing, the last portion—because of these paved interrupters— is where the most concentration is necessary. In a more pleasing vein, you also pass a man-made pond that is home to ducks, geese, kingfishers, herons, raccoons, fox, beaver, and deer. Shortly thereafter, you reach the Upper Overlook parking lot.

HIGHLIGHTS

There is a wealth of activity alternatives for non-running visitors to Lake Lanier. Maps for the Laurel Ridge Trail are available at the Lanier Project Management Office (one parking lot away from the Upper Overlook). Although not plentiful, the lake and dam views are amazing.

KEEP IN MIND

Pets are not allowed on the Laurel Ridge Trail—not even on leashes. When on the Chattahoochee River section of the trail, users should take the higher ground prior to water releases from the Buford Dam; a warning horn will sound before the actual release. Release schedules can be found by listening to 1610 AM on the radio or by calling 770-945-1466. Other information about the trail or the surrounding area is available from the Lanier Project Management Office at P.O. Box 567, Buford, GA 30315. The telephone number is 770-945-9531.

NEARBY NOTABLES

There are a few convenience stores near the parking lot where you can purchase snacks and drinks. The most enjoyable option would be to bring a picnic basket and cooler for dining on the scenic park grounds.

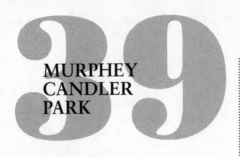

MURPHEY CANDLER PARK

DISTANCE
2.0 miles, 3.2 kilometers (loop)

HILL FACTOR
Mild

GETTING THERE
Approximately 12 miles northeast of downtown. Take I-285 to Ashford Dunwoody Road (exit 29) and go south to West Nancy Creek Drive, then east to the park.

PARKING
There is a large parking lot at the corner of West Nancy Creek and Thomas Road, where the trailhead is located. On summer weekends, parking may be scarce because of Little League. Other parking lots are located nearby, and parking is permitted on most side streets off West Nancy Creek.

PUBLIC TRANSPORTATION
The area is served by the Chamblee/Donaldson (#29) MARTA bus, which departs from the Chamblee Station.

OVERVIEW
If you are not sure trail running is for you and you need a place to find out, or if you are a trail runner who can't find an in-town trail free of congestion, or if you are looking for a course suitable for laps or speed work—look no further. Murphey Candler Park fits the bill perfectly. The trail is challenging and uneven at times, but it is largely free of rocks and unexpected chasms.

THE COURSE
MAIN ROUTE: This is an off-road trail around Murphey Candler Lake. Regardless of which direction you go from the starting point on West Nancy Creek Drive, the trail starts out wide and eventually becomes a single track. The portion of the route farthest from the road is shaded by many trees. The trail crosses two footbridges, climbs a few short but steep hills, and makes some surprising but fun and impossible to miss turns. The last 0.25-mile consists of sidewalks near a picnic area and along West Nancy Creek Road.

HIGHLIGHTS
Mileage is marked every 0.25 mile. The lake is home to

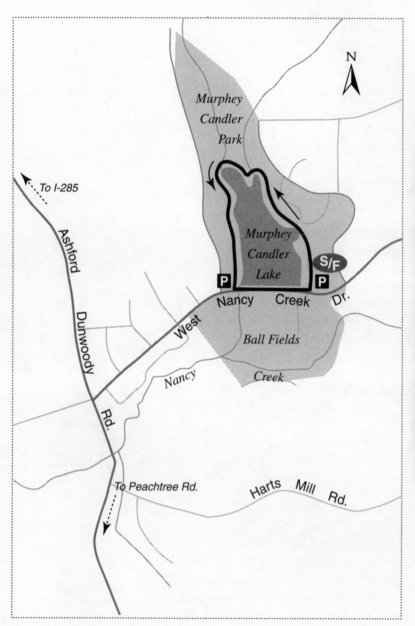

N

Murphey
Candler
Park

To I-285

Ashford

Dunwoody

Murphey
Candler
Lake

S/F

P   P

Nancy   Creek   Dr.

West

Nancy

Ball Fields

Creek

Rd.

To Peachtree Rd.

Harts   Mill   Rd.

167

various local and migrating fowl,
easily seen from many vantage
points along the trail.

KEEP IN MIND

Others use the trail for
leisurely strolls or walks with dogs.
Because of the proximity of the
lake, this trail seems to hold water
and mud after heavy rains longer
than most.

NEARBY NOTABLES

Plenty of picnic spaces and
grills are available for non-runners.
During the summer and on
evenings and weekends you can
enjoy a cookout while watching a
Little League Baseball game after
your workout. There are three
fields for organized games across
from the park.

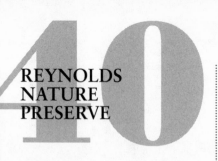

REYNOLDS NATURE PRESERVE

DISTANCE
1.5 miles, 2.4 kilometers (loop)

HILL FACTOR
Moderate

GETTING THERE
Approximately 10 miles southeast of downtown. Take I-75 to Jonesboro Road/GA 54 (exit 233) and go north to Reynolds Road, then west to the Reynolds Preserve Nature Center.

PARKING
Plenty of free parking is available in the lot at the Nature Center. There is additional parking in another preserve lot 0.5 mile east of the Nature Center.

PUBLIC TRANSPORTATION
The area is served by C-TRAN (Clayton Country Transit) bus #501, which departs from the Airport MARTA Station.

OVERVIEW
The 146-acre William Reynolds Nature Preserve is an attractive option for certain trail runners. The even, relatively hazard-free trails are perfect for anyone who is trying off-road running for the first time, striving to improve footwork, or simply looking for serenity. The short loop distance and the typically light trail usage make this an enticing option for those who want to enhance their trail-running abilities by performing speed work and timing splits. On the other hand, if you just want to go, and then go farther, this is not a good option.

THE COURSE
MAIN ROUTE: Begin on the trailhead that extends from the Nature Center. Because it is a loop, you can go in either direction. If you go right (northwest) from the trailhead, you quickly come upon the Reynolds Farm. As you pass the barn, other outbuildings, and compost area, you begin going south. There are no mile markers, but when you pass the 0.5-mile point, you will see additional trail options. In order to complete this loop, always follow the outermost trail, which goes through woodlands and wetlands where wildlife is frequently visible. The last 0.75 mile takes you by a series of ponds.

REYNOLDS NATURE PRESERVE

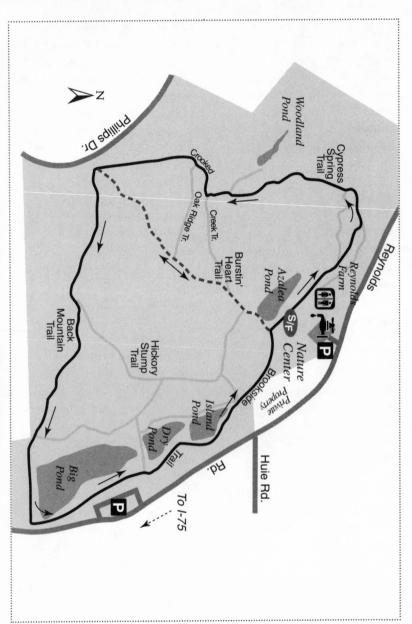

ALTERNATE: Another 2.5 miles of trails crisscross each other within the interior of the loop and are equally user-friendly. If you desire more challenging ascents, be sure to conquer the Burstin' Heart trail at least once. This trail is identified by signage on the outer loop trail and is well marked on the posted maps.

HIGHLIGHTS
The trails are wide, soft, and almost entirely free of hazards. It is virtually impossible to get lost. There is a trail map on the information board at the trailhead.

KEEP IN MIND
The preserve is open only until dusk. Conditions can be muddy on some trails after heavy rains because of the proximity of wetlands. The Nature Center is open Monday–Friday, 8:30 AM– 5:30 PM. For information on conditions, call 770-603-4188.

NEARBY NOTABLES
On GA Highway 54, there are a large number of fast food establishments and gas stations with convenience centers.

41 COCHRAN MILL NATURE CENTER and PARK

DISTANCE
4.0 miles, 6.4 kilometers (loop)

HILL FACTOR
Moderate

GETTING THERE
Approximately 26 miles southwest of downtown. Take I-85 to South Fulton Parkway (exit 68) and go southwest to Rivertown Road, then west to Cochran Mill Road, then southeast to the Nature Center.

PARKING
Parking is available at the nature center for those who have made the minimum $1.00 contribution. Plenty of free parking is available at the park.

PUBLIC TRANSPORTATION
There is no public transportation in this area.

OVERVIEW
Cochran Mill Park is managed by Fulton County Parks and Recreation, and the Cochran Mill Nature Center is operated by a private, nonprofit group as a nature preserve and animal rehabilitation center. These unique neighbors come together to provide local trail runners with the perfect blend of off-road conditions and natural scenery.

THE COURSE
MAIN ROUTE: This route begins at the Cochran Mill Nature Center. The trail starts behind the center with an "am-I-ready-for-this?" hill that ascends less than 0.25 mile to the top. Continue south for the next 0.5 mile along the narrow trail over Still Creek and an old logging road. As you begin a westward descent toward Bear Creek, a dramatic view of the marshy bog area below greets you.

Follow the trail along Bear Creek. At the rock outcropping, the Nature Center Trail scrambles *up* to its conclusion. For a more lengthy run, scramble *down* to the path that continues along the creek. A little more than 0.25 mile along the waterway, cross the footbridge into Cochran Mill Park and head back in the direction you just came. You're now on the opposite side of Bear Creek. Follow this trail almost 0.5 mile, past the old grist mill dam to the first trail after the dam that

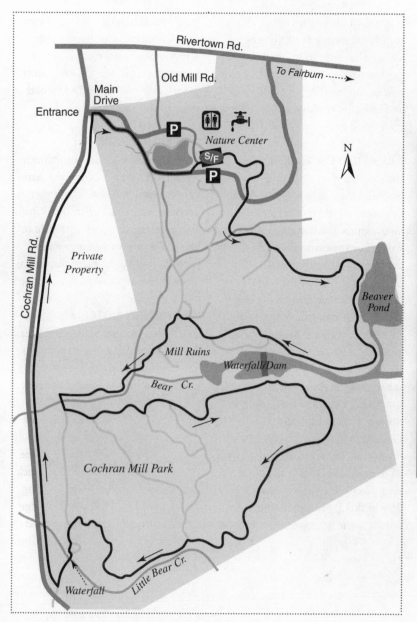

Rivertown Rd.

Old Mill Rd.

To Fairburn ------▶

Main Drive

Entrance

P

Nature Center

S/F

P

N

Cochran Mill Rd.

Private Property

Beaver Pond

Mill Ruins

Waterfall/Dam

Bear Cr.

Cochran Mill Park

Little Bear Cr.

Waterfall

goes south (or to the right). This turn is not marked with blazes or signs and is easy to miss; you won't experience any significant risks if you miss it, as the path soon ends and you can turn around and re-trace your steps.

Leaving Bear Creek, run through heavy forest on a wide trail. Disregard all spur (narrow) trails along this path. A little more than 0.25 mile later, as you come to Little Bear Creek, the trail meanders west (or to the right). Although the trail concludes at the base of the waterfall on Little Bear Creek near an old iron bridge, your adventure does not. The bridge is closed to any type of crossing, so make your way across the water by *carefully* using the dry, stable rocks in the creek to reach the other side. Once safely across, take the short road out of the park to Cochran Mill Road and turn right (or north). The wide, soft shoulder of the road provides ample room to finish your off-road trek. Make your way back 1.0 mile, predominantly uphill, to the nature center entrance.

HIGHLIGHTS
The scenery is diverse and remarkable. Be sure to visit the nature center to learn about the plants and wildlife that are indigenous to the area.

KEEP IN MIND
The nature center is open from 9:00 AM to 3:00 PM; the park is open until 9:00 PM. The rock outcroppings can be wet and slick. It is best to avoid this park after heavy rains. The trails contain potential hazards such as roots, rocks, and uneven footing.

NEARBY NOTABLES
The Cochran Mill Nature Center provides a rest room, drinking fountain, and drink-vending machines.

THE PEACHTREE ROAD RACE

US 10K CLASSIC

ATLANTA MARATHON

AND HALF MARATHON

THE PEACHTREE ROAD RACE

DATE
Independence Day

DISTANCE
6.2 miles, 10.0 kilometers

HILL FACTOR
Moderate

GETTING THERE

The starting point of this race is at Lenox Square, 6.5 miles northeast of downtown. Take I-285 to GA 400 South (exit 27) to the Buckhead Loop (exit 2) and go east to Peachtree Road.

PARKING

Parking is available in the commercial lots along the course before the road closes very early the morning of the race. Parking is also available in the residential areas on both sides of Peachtree north of the Peachtree Dunwoody intersection. This is an attractive option if you have a higher entry number and are starting toward the back of the pack—which is spread out to the

north and closer to this intersection. Parking is also allowed on most streets around Piedmont Park (where the finish line is located) and in the surrounding neighborhoods. Parking is very scarce as the starting time nears.

PUBLIC TRANSPORTATION

The best option for both runners and spectators is to take MARTA. Both the Lenox and Buckhead Stations are within easy walking distance of the starting point at Lenox Square. The Arts Center and Midtown Stations are reasonably close to the finish line. MARTA runs extra trains before, during, and after the race to handle the large number of riders.

OVERVIEW

This Fourth of July tradition, dating back to 1970, has the largest number of participants of any 10K race in the world. Almost 60,000 runners, many from the metropolitan Atlanta area, accept the Atlanta Track Club's invitation. Were it not for capacity considerations, the numbers would be even greater, as thousands of additional entries are rejected every year.

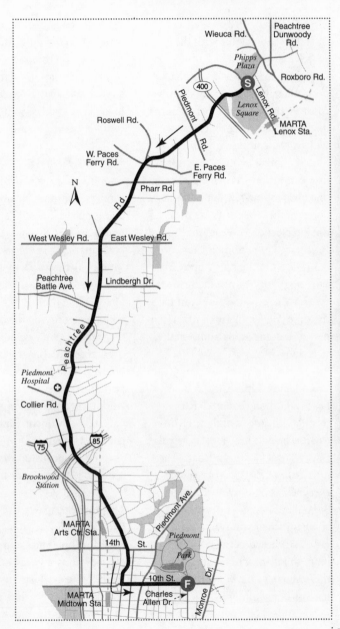

THE COURSE

The race begins with the wheelchair division at 7:00 AM at Lenox Square in Buckhead. Runners officially start at 7:30, but because of the large number of participants, real starting times vary widely. Depending on your entry number and starting position, you may not actually cross the starting line until as much as an hour later. Some runners begin as far north as the intersection of Peachtree and Peachtree Dunwoody Roads, over 0.5 mile from the race's official starting point. As you inch slowly southward, however, you can pass the time conversing with other runners and doing some additional stretching.

From Lenox Square, the course heads south on Peachtree Road through Buckhead and into Midtown. The first mile is relatively flat as you cross Piedmont Road. The next 2.0 miles offer a pleasant and ever-increasing downward slope. At 3.0 miles, what goes down must come up when you reach "Cardiac Hill," so named because of its proximity to Piedmont Hospital. After this steep 0.5 mile climb, the route flattens out again until mile 5.0. Just south of the High Museum of Art, a gradual ascent begins and continues for close to 0.5 mile and the left turn onto Tenth Street. This turn provides a relatively flat homestretch into Piedmont Park, the finish line, and the well-deserved reception that await you.

HIGHLIGHTS

If you think the number of runners is impressive, imagine this: an estimated 200,000 spectators line Peachtree Road to cheer their participating friends and family. Many businesses along Peachtree open early to lend a festive atmosphere to the race. Every year 3,000 volunteers provide for the needs of the runners. Well-managed aid stations are available at every mile offering water, sports drinks, and portable toilets. In fact, the volunteers and race organizers painstakingly ensure that participants get not only the fluids, but also the support that they need in order to get to the finish line.

The post-race party in Piedmont Park is second to none, with music, refreshments, and plenty of other people happy to hear how you fared. Most importantly, after crossing the finish line, you will be directed to the pick-up point for your race T-shirt—one of Atlanta's most recognizable articles of clothing and a fashion statement.

KEEP IN MIND

Even early in the morning in July, it can be extremely hot and humid in Atlanta. The course route is closed in the morning prior to the race, making it tricky for automobiles to get around in the nearby areas. Allow adequate time and then add fifteen minutes to get to the race. It is highly recommended that you use MARTA for pre- and post-race transportation. If you do drive to the start, you must make your own arrangements to get back to the start to retrieve your car and other belongings. Because of the number of participants, this is not a race you should enter with the mindset of achieving a new personal record. Unless they start near the front, speed demons only frustrate themselves and others while trying to hastily negotiate their way through the throngs of their fellow runners.

HOW TO ENTER

The highly anticipated official entry form is published in the *Atlanta Journal-Constitution* on the third Sunday in March. If you are out of town or you prefer to handle your entry by mail, you may send a stamped, self-addressed envelope to the Atlanta Track Club, 3097 East Shadowlawn Avenue, Atlanta, GA 30305. They will mail you an application so that it arrives about the same time the form is published in the newspaper.

Fill out the form and put it in the mail *immediately*, along with the required copy of a valid form of identification. Despite the fact that the post office is closed on Sunday, many determined runners will make a trip anyway to ensure an early postmark date, a good tip to hasten your entry's arrival to the Atlanta Track Club. Entries are accepted by United States Postal Service only and are accepted in order of postmark date; each year many applicants are turned away. As of this printing, the entry fee is $25.00. For more information, visit the Atlanta Track Club's website at www.atlantatrackclub.org.

43

US 10K CLASSIC

DATE
Labor Day

DISTANCE
6.2 miles, 10.0 kilometers

HILL FACTOR
Significant

GETTING THERE
Approximately 11.0 miles northwest of downtown. Take I-285 to South Cobb Drive/US 41 (exit 19) and go south to the Cobb Galleria Centre.

PARKING
Plenty of parking is available at the Galleria. Plan to arrive at least thirty minutes before the race start in order to get into the lots.

PUBLIC TRANSPORTATION
The Cobb Galleria Centre is served by the #10 Cobb County Transit (CCT) bus, which departs from the Arts Center MARTA Station. CCT provides a free shuttle

from the finish line back to the starting point.

OVERVIEW
If you believe that you should labor on Labor Day, enter the US 10K Classic. Touting itself as "America's Greatest 10K," this race serves up a generous portion of long, steep hills to test your oxygen capacity. From the Cobb Galleria Centre to White Water Park, this race is run entirely on the wide, not terribly scenic, usually congested US 41. It won't take long for even the newest runner to figure out why this route did not make the *Atlanta Running Guide* on its own merit. However, the event organization, participant numbers, and worthy cause (proceeds are donated to designated children's charities) make this a favorite of 10,000-meter aficionados.

THE COURSE
The starter's gun goes off at 7:20 AM for in-line skaters; the wheelchair division begins ten minutes later. Runners complete the staggered start at 7:45 AM. After a brief descent away from the Galleria and underneath I-285, your first ascent begins; it's only 0.3 mile, but it seems like twice that because of

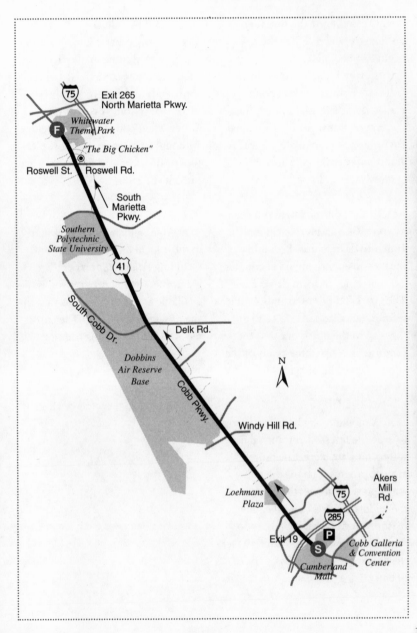

the hill's grade. At the top, there is no time to celebrate, for the descent begins immediately, down a slope that is every bit as steep as the hill you just climbed. At this point, you realize that the initial hill was just the first of many. Another of equal challenge lies immediately ahead, and it appears that others follow endlessly.

At mile 2.0, things flatten out a bit as you pass a series of strip malls and auto dealerships. Beginning at the 4.0-mile marker, you encounter another series of formidable climbs. The last 1.2 miles offer undulating terrain, but gradually descend all the way to the finish line and the promise of a dip in the pools of the White Water theme park.

HIGHLIGHTS
Although potentially punishing to even the fittest of entrants, the rolling hills are a great measure of athletic progress. This is the only way you will ever get to run down the middle of US 41 and the only reason you would ever want to. Admission to the Six Flags White Water theme park is included in the price of entry.

KEEP IN MIND
Do any other comments about the hills need to be made? To save time and money, purchase tickets for friends and family members who wish to join you at White Water when you submit your entry. Although spectators are most plentiful at the start and finish, they are present the entire way.

HOW TO ENTER
An application can be found in most local fitness publications, including *Atlanta Sports & Fitness* magazine. Online registration is available at the organization's website at www.us10k.org. The entry fee is $25.00 as of this printing.

44

ATLANTA MARATHON & HALF MARATHON

DATE
Thanksgiving Day

DISTANCE
26.2 miles and 13.1 miles,
42.0 and 21.0 kilometers

HILL FACTOR
Significant

GETTING THERE

The marathon starts at Turner Field, approximately 1.0 mile south of downtown. Take I-75/I-85 to Fulton Street (exit 246) and go west on Capitol Avenue.

The half marathon starts at Peachtree Industrial Boulevard and Malone Drive, on the north side of Atlanta, approximately 11.0 miles from downtown Atlanta. Take I-285 to Peachtree Industrial Boulevard (exit 31), and go south.

PARKING

Plenty of parking is available in the Turner Field lots for the marathon—and for this occasion,

it's free. Parking for the half marathon is available in the commercial lots along Peachtree Industrial Boulevard.

PUBLIC TRANSPORTATION

Turner Field is located just a few blocks from the Georgia State MARTA Station.

The intersection of Peachtree Industrial Boulevard and Malone Drive is one block east of the Chamblee MARTA Station.

OVERVIEW

The Atlanta Marathon has been held on Thanksgiving for more than twenty years. One of the ten oldest marathons in the United States, it covers nearly 90 percent of the course used for the 1996 Centennial Olympic Games marathon. The half marathon is the country's third largest, attracting nearly 7,000 runners; the full marathon traditionally draws about 1,000 competitors. To accommodate the runners and respect the holiday schedule of the volunteers, the races begin in early morning—the half marathon at 7:00 AM and the full at 7:30. Conveniently, the half marathon is run on the same course as the last 13.0 miles of the

THE ATLANTA MARATHON/
HALF MARATHON

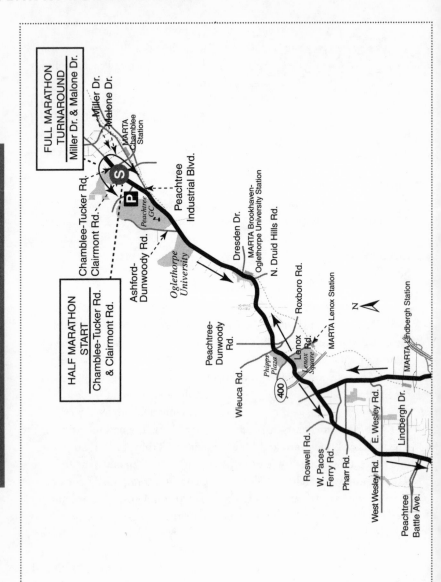

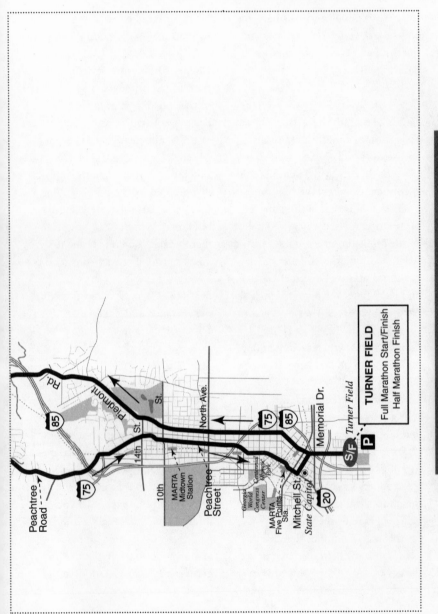

THE ATLANTA MARATHON/
HALF MARATHON

full marathon. Not surprisingly, the courses are very hilly, and most of the distance is primarily run on Peachtree Road.

THE COURSE

The marathon starts at Turner Field, home of the Atlanta Braves, and heads north to Piedmont Road. "The Early Riser," the first hill you encounter, is merely the beginning of a series of hills that become more pronounced over the next 7.0 miles. While on Piedmont, you pass such Atlanta landmarks as Piedmont Park, the Atlanta Botanical Garden, and Fat Matt's Rib Shack, a local barbecue favorite. After reaching the summit of the "Hill Too Pharr" (Road, that is) you leave Piedmont and go north on Peachtree Road.

Once on Peachtree Road, the route rolls gently north past Lenox Square and Phipps Plaza, where many spectators gather. As you head into Brookhaven, you begin to see the lead runners who have already made the midpoint turnaround. Try not to be discouraged—the purse for this race is not that significant. This is also the flattest stretch of the course. After the Ashford Dunwoody intersection at the 10.5-mile mark, there are only two moderate hills that stand between you and the turn, located just past Malone Drive.

Malone Drive is the starting point for half marathoners. The remainder of the course is almost all on Peachtree Road, with the exception of the final mile, which incorporates Mitchell Street and Capitol Avenue. The hill on Mitchell, aptly dubbed "Capital Punishment" because it takes you past the State Capitol building, is your last climb. From there, make your way home to Turner Field. The races finish on relatively flat Capitol Avenue underneath the Olympic Rings that mark the entrance into the former Olympic Stadium.

HIGHLIGHTS

More than in other marathons, and maybe because of the holiday, there is great camaraderie among the participants in this race. Because of the simplicity of the route, it is easy for friends and family members with cars and working knowledge of some side streets to see you at multiple points along the course. And there is just something marvelous about finishing under an archway of gold-plated Olympic rings.

KEEP IN MIND

Although certain streets close for the race as starting time approaches, volunteers are present to direct you. Weather in Atlanta in November is unpredictable; sun, rain, sleet, snow and temperatures anywhere from the teens to the sixties have all been part of the forecast in the past. The crowd support is understandably light because of ongoing turkey preparations.

HOW TO ENTER

An application can be found in most local fitness publications, including *Atlanta Sports & Fitness* magazine. You can also visit the Atlanta Track Club website at www.atlantatrackclub.org to complete an online registration. Entry fees are $40.00 for the full marathon and $30.00 for the half marathon as of this printing. As a way to discourage last-minute decisions, entry fees balloon to $65.00 and $55.00 respectively if you register late (usually anytime within three weeks of the race).

Appendix A

ALPHABETICAL LISTING

ALPHABETICAL LISTING

Appendix B

DISTANCE

The categories below refer to each route's main run(s) only. Please see each chapter description for options for extending or decreasing the length of your run.

(CRNRA refers to the Chattahoochee River National Recreation Area.)

DISTANCE:
1.0 TO 3.1 MILES

Reynolds
   Nature Preserve..............1.5 miles
Piedmont Park/
   Midtown..............1.5 to 2.0 miles
Drew Valley.......................1.7 miles
Murphey Candler Park......2.0 miles
CRNRA West Palisades.....2.5 miles
CRNRA Johnson
   Ferry North....................2.5 miles
CRNRA East Palisades......3.0 miles
CRNRA Jones Bridge........3.0 miles
Brookhaven ....3.0 miles
Avondale Estates................3.0 miles
Sweetwater Creek ....3.0 miles
CRNRA Cochran Shoals...3.1 miles

DISTANCE:
3.2 TO 6.2 MILES

Virginia-Highland..............3.2 miles
CRNRA Bowmans Island..3.2 miles

CRNRA Island Ford........3.25 miles
Peachtree City..................3.25 miles
Mason Mill......................3.75 miles
Chastain Park ....4.0 miles
Wieuca Road ....4.0 miles
Grant Park/
   Oakland Cemetery........4.0 miles
CRNRA West Palisades.....4.0 miles
Cochran Mill Nature Center
   and Park ....4.0 miles
CRNRA Vickery Creek ...4.25 miles
CRNRA Gold Branch........4.5 miles
Garden Hills
   and Peachtree Hills ....4.5 miles
East Cobb ....5.0 miles
Westview Cemetery ....5.0 miles
Freedom Parkway Trail .....5.0 miles
Sagamore Hills ....5.0 miles
Kennesaw Mountain...........5.0 miles
CRNRA East Palisades......5.0 miles
Sweetwater Creek ....5.0 miles
Stone Mountain Park.........5.0 miles
Marietta.............................5.0 miles
Downtown Atlanta.............5.0 miles
North Fayette ....5.0 miles
Ansley Park
   and Morningside............5.5 miles
Red Top Mountain ....5.5 miles
Decatur..............................5.75 miles
West Paces Ferry Road ......6.0 miles
Vinings ....6.0 miles
Sandy Springs ....6.0 miles
CRNRA Jones Bridge........6.0 miles
Roswell..............................6.0 miles
Lilburn..............................6.0 miles

Alpharetta ....6.2 miles

DISTANCE:
6.3 TO 10.0 MILES
Buckhead ....6.5 miles
North Fayette....................6.5 miles
Peachtree Dunwoody ....7.0 miles
Ponce de Leon Corridor ....8.0 miles
Emory/Druid Hills.............8.0 miles
Stone Mountain ....8.0 miles
Kennesaw Mountain ....10.0 miles

DISTANCE:
GREATER THAN 10.0 MILES
Peachtree Road ....11.0 miles
Mount Paran....................11.0 miles
Roswell ....11.5 miles
Kennesaw Mountain
    (long loop) ....16.0 miles
The Silver Comet Trail ...25.6 miles

Appendix C

HILL FACTOR

(CRNRA refers to the Chattahoochee River National Recreation Area.)

Appendix D

RUN BY TYPE

(CRNRA refers to the Chattahoochee River National Recreation Area.)

Appendix E

AUTHOR'S TOP PICKS

(CRNRA refers to the Chattahoochee River National Recreation Area.)

SHOWER AND SHAMPOO SPECIALS (BEST CHANCES FOR GETTING DIRTY)

FAST ACTION (BEST COURSES FOR SPEED WORK)

EASY LIVING (BEST COURSES TO RUN AND RELAX)

Appendix F
RUNNING CLUBS

Atlanta Hash House
   Harriers and Harriettes
770-455-6952
404-377-2888
www.atlantahash.com

Atlanta Singles
   Running Organization
404-657-3824
www.atlanta-singles-running.org

Atlanta Track Club
404-231-9064
www.atlantatrackclub.org

Brookhaven Area Runners
404-233-4242

Chattahoochee Road Runners
770-980-9239
http://www.crrclub.com/

Front Runners Atlanta (gay/lesbian)
770-621-5007
www.frontrunnersatlanta.org

Galloway Training Group
   (running groups and
   training programs)
404-255-1033
www.jeffgalloway.com

Georgia Orienteering Club
404-366-3396
www.gaorienteering.org

Godspeed Running Club (Christian)
770-518-8932
770-343-8585

Kennesaw Ultra Distance Runners
770-590-1567

Joints in Motion (Training Group)
The Arthritis Foundation
404-237-8771
www.arthritis.org

Marietta Runners' Club
770-427-4471

Midtown Runners
404-875-9602

Peachtree City Running Club
770-631-7658
www.ptcrc.com

Roswell Runners' Club
770-451-5500
www.roswellrunners.com

South DeKalb Striders
404-284-7986

South Fulton Running Partners
404-755-9528
sfrp@accessatlanta.com

Team Diabetes (Training Group)
American Diabetes Association
888-342-2383
www.diabetes.org

Team in Training (Training Group)
The Leukemia & Lymphoma Society
770-438-6006
www.teamtraining.org

Team Spirit (Training Group)
Running for Humanity
404-355-5833
www.teamspiritrunners.org

Windward (Alpharetta) Runners
770-360-5700

RUNNING CLUBS

Appendix G

RUNNING PACE CHART

min/mile	2 miles	3 miles	5K	3.5 miles	5 miles	6 miles	10K	15K
4:45	9:30	14:15	14:45	16:38	23:45	28:30	29:31	44:16
5:00	10:00	15:00	15:32	17:30	25:00	30:00	31:04	46:36
5:15	10:30	15:45	16:19	18:22	26:15	31:30	32:37	48:56
5:30	11:00	16:30	17:05	19:15	27:30	33:00	34:11	51:16
5:45	11:30	17:15	17:52	20:08	28:45	34:30	35:44	53:36
6:00	12:00	18:00	18:38	21:00	30:00	36:00	37:17	55:55
6:15	12:30	18:45	19:25	21:53	31:15	37:30	38:50	58:15
6:30	13:00	19:30	20:12	22:45	32:30	39:00	40:23	1:00:35
6:45	13:30	20:15	20:58	23:37	33:45	40:30	41:57	1:02:55
7:00	14:00	21:00	21:45	24:30	35:00	42:00	43:30	1:05:15
7:15	14:30	21:45	22:31	25:22	36:15	43:30	45:03	1:07:34
7:30	15:00	22:30	23:18	26:15	37:30	45:00	46:36	1:09:54
7:45	15:30	23:15	24:05	27:08	38:45	46:30	48:09	1:12:14
8:00	16:00	24:00	24:51	28:00	40:00	48:00	49:43	1:14:34
8:15	16:30	24:45	25:38	28:53	41:15	49:30	51:16	1:16:54
8:30	17:00	25:30	26:24	29:45	42:30	51:00	52:49	1:19:13
8:45	17:30	26:15	27:11	30:37	43:45	52:30	54:22	1:21:33
9:00	18:00	27:00	27:58	31:30	45:00	54:00	55:55	1:23:53
9:15	18:30	27:45	28:44	32:23	46:15	55:30	57:29	1:26:13
9:30	19:00	28:30	29:31	33:15	47:30	57:00	59:02	1:28:33
9:45	19:30	29:15	30:18	34:07	48:45	58:30	1:00:35	1:30:53
10:00	20:00	30:00	31:04	35:00	50:00	1:00:00	1:02:08	1:33:12
10:30	21:00	31:30	32:37	36:45	52:30	1:03:00	1:05:15	1:37:52
11:00	22:00	33:00	34:11	38:30	55:00	1:06:00	1:08:21	1:42:32
11:30	23:00	34:30	35:44	40:15	57:30	1:09:00	1:11:27	1:47:11
12:00	24:00	36:00	37:17	42:00	1:00:00	1:12:00	1:14:34	1:51:51

min/ mile	10 miles	20K	half marathon	15 miles	25K	30K	20 miles	full marathon
4:45	47:30	59:02	1:02:16	1:11:15	1:13:47	1:28:33	1:35:00	2:04:32
5:00	50:00	1:02:08	1:05:33	1:15:00	1:17:40	1:33:12	1:40:00	2:11:06
5:15	52:30	1:05:15	1:08:49	1:18:45	1:21:33	1:37:52	1:45:00	2:17:39
5:30	55:00	1:08:21	1:12:06	1:22:30	1:25:26	1:42:32	1:50:00	2:24:12
5:45	57:30	1:11:27	1:15:23	1:26:15	1:29:19	1:47:11	1:55:00	2:30:45
6:00	1:00:00	1:14:34	1:18:39	1:30:00	1:33:12	1:51:51	2:00:00	2:37:19
6:15	1:02:30	1:17:40	1:21:56	1:33:45	1:37:05	1:56:30	2:05:00	2:43:52
6:30	1:05:00	1:20:47	1:25:13	1:37:30	1:40:58	2:01:10	2:10:00	2:50:25
6:45	1:07:30	1:23:53	1:28:29	1:41:15	1:44:51	2:05:50	2:15:00	2:56:59
7:00	1:10:00	1:27:00	1:31:46	1:45:00	1:48:44	2:10:29	2:20:00	3:03:32
7:15	1:12:30	1:30:06	1:35:03	1:48:45	1:52:37	2:15:09	2:25:00	3:10:05
7:30	1:15:00	1:33:12	1:38:19	1:52:30	1:56:30	2:19:49	2:30:00	3:16:38
7:45	1:17:30	1:36:19	1:41:36	1:56:15	2:00:23	2:24:28	2:35:00	3:23:12
8:00	1:20:00	1:39:25	1:44:53	2:00:00	2:04:16	2:29:08	2:40:00	3:29:45
8:15	1:22:30	1:42:32	1:48:09	2:03:45	2:08:09	2:33:47	2:45:00	3:36:18
8:30	1:25:00	1:45:38	1:51:26	2:07:30	2:12:02	2:38:27	2:50:00	3:42:52
8:45	1:27:30	1:48:44	1:54:42	2:11:15	2:15:55	2:43:07	2:55:00	3:49:25
9:00	1:30:00	1:51:51	1:57:59	2:15:00	2:19:49	2:47:46	3:00:00	3:55:58
9:15	1:32:30	1:54:57	2:01:16	2:18:45	2:23:42	2:52:26	3:05:00	4:02:31
9:30	1:35:00	1:58:04	2:04:32	2:22:30	2:27:35	2:57:05	3:10:00	4:09:05
9:45	1:37:30	2:01:10	2:07:49	2:26:15	2:31:28	3:01:45	3:15:00	4:15:38
10:00	1:40:00	2:04:16	2:11:06	2:30:00	2:35:21	3:06:25	3:20:00	4:22:11
10:30	1:45:00	2:10:29	2:17:39	2:37:30	2:43:07	3:15:44	3:30:00	4:35:18
11:00	1:50:00	2:16:42	2:24:12	2:45:00	2:50:53	3:25:03	3:40:00	4:48:24
11:30	1:55:00	2:22:55	2:30:45	2:52:30	2:58:39	3:34:22	3:50:00	5:01:31
12:00	2:00:00	2:29:08	2:37:19	3:00:00	3:06:25	3:43:42	4:00:00	5:14:37

Mike Cosentino

A **veteran of** more than thirty marathons, Mike has recently earned top-three finishes in the Calloway Gardens (GA) Marathon, the Dutchess County Classic (NY) Marathon, the Louisville (KY) Marathon, and the Crater Lake Rim (OR) Marathon. A former *Atlanta Sports & Fitness* magazine's "Athlete of the Year," he has also completed a number of ultras, including the Kettle Moraine (WI) 100 Miler, the Western States (CA) 100-Mile Endurance Run, the Leadville (CO) 100-Mile "Race Across The Sky," and the Ironman Florida Triathlon. Mike received a Bachelor of Science degree from Vanderbilt University and a Masters in Sports Administration from Ohio University.

Originally from Elkhart, Indiana, Mike Cosentino now calls Atlanta home, having lived here for almost ten years. He lives in Brookhaven with his wife, Inge, their son, Campbell, and their three dogs.

A Note to my Fellow Runners in Atlanta

WHEN I read and re-read the original manuscript, I always felt good. I wanted to go for a run. I hope this book makes you feel the same way.

When you decide to go out and try a new or unfamiliar run listed in the *Atlanta Running Guide*, keep in mind that running is an adventure. It is the original extreme sport. It was "X" before "X" was cool. The preceding pages, no matter how helpful, will not decrease your chances of spraining your ankle, being chased by a dog, or getting hit by a maniacal driver in an overpriced SUV.

Keep in mind that Atlanta is quite hilly and can be very hot. I warn you about conditions where I can but each runner possesses a different skill level and willingness to accept discomfort. If you want a guarantee of consistent shade and flat terrain, buy a treadmill.

I have tried to be unbiased and thoughtful in my recommendations,

with the whims of my fellow Atlanta runners always on my mind. But I am human...and I cannot accept responsibility for any inconveniences, injuries, or incorrect information you may encounter.

Another consideration...a bit of advice, if you will: Don't always (or strictly) follow the directions on these pages. When you are out for a run, get a little lost, follow your curiosity, and fulfill your desire to discover something new. When you do, I would be honored if you let me know about it. Your feedback, suggestions, and updates will be the most important element in improving future editions of the *Atlanta Running Guide*.

Lastly, please be careful out there.... After all, sprained ankles hurt, some dogs have bites worse than their bark, and collisions with SUVs just plain take the fun out of running.

Happy trails!

Mike Cosentino
c/o Peachtree Publishers
1700 Chattahoochee Avenue
Atlanta, GA 30318-2112
atlantaruns@hotmail.com

AUTHOR'S NOTE

The Peachtree Road Race starting line at Lenox Square.